Your Investment Advisor is Wrong!

The Conventional Wisdom Used by Most
Advisors to Protect & Grow Your Assets
Hasn't Worked, Doesn't Work & Won't Work!

Learn the superior way to save and
invest in any economic environment*

By Harry M. Beck, CFA, CFP®, CLU

*The little-known and less costly method of managing
money that *allows you to sleep at night*

Your Investment Advisor is Wrong!

Harry M. Beck

©Harry M. Beck 2012

Published by 1stWorld Publishing

P.O. Box 2211, Fairfield, Iowa 52556

tel: 641-209-5000 • fax: 866-440-5234

web: www.1stworldpublishing.com

First Edition

LCCN: 201293324

SoftCover ISBN: 978-1-4218-8643-5

HardCover ISBN: 978-1-4218-8644-2

eBook ISBN: 978-1-4218-8645-9

TABLE OF CONTENTS

DEDICATION

This book is dedicated to the unknown individual who created the oldest and most famous joke about Wall Street. It goes something like this:

A father is on the top floor of an Ivory Tower on Wall Street showing his young son the view of New York Harbor.

"Look at those magnificent yachts over there!" said the father to his son. "They belong to the bankers."

"Do you see the yachts on the other side of the harbor?" continued the man, "They belong to the brokers."

The son thought for a while, turned to his father and asked, "But Daddy, where are the customers' yachts?"

CHAPTER 1

INTRODUCTION

In October 2008, the world's financial markets crashed. Most institutional and individual financial advisors, particularly those who believed in diversifying risk through "asset allocation," saw their clients' portfolios drop by unimagined amounts. At least fourteen trillion dollars in equity (stock) valuation—not just a few hundred billion—was lost. Hard assets (particularly gold), other commodities, private equity investments, and fixed income—all of which were presumed "uncorrelated" or "lowly correlated" to equities—collapsed with the decline of stocks and real estate. With the exception of Treasury bonds, considered a deflation hedge, no asset class was spared. Clients—people like you and me—lost many nights of sleep wondering what happened and what to do next.

It turns out 2008 was not the only bad time period for many investors. During the previous ten years, stocks lost 4% compounded and underperformed the safest investment in the world: U.S. Treasury bills. Treasury bills—low yielding because of their safety—outperformed stocks! This makes some people believe the period from 2000 to 2008 was merely a "bear market rally." Yet the standard financial advice, the "conventional wisdom," was and is to "asset allocate" for diversification, and to hold onto stock and bond investments for the long run. The rationale for this advice is: (1) Asset allocation models diversify your portfolio and minimize investment risk; and (2) Stocks earn 10%-12% per year over the long run. Some of the best and the brightest marketers in the financial services industry based their business practices on this collective thinking or "conventional wisdom." As we will learn later in this book, the "conventional wisdom," was and is wrong.

However flawed, the "conventional wisdom" seems to prevail. From the ivory towers of the institutional trust companies and large brokerage firms to the housewife-turned-financial-planner hanging a shingle outside her modest apartment, the "conventional wisdom" is pervasive in the financial industry. It was taught in almost every corporate training program and to candidates of every industry certification or designation (e.g., CERTIFIED FINANCIAL PLANNER™ certification, Chartered Life Underwriter, etc.). Retail brokers working for Merrill Lynch, UBS, Goldman Sachs, Morgan Stanley, Smith Barney, Edward Jones, and others based their business models around the conventional wisdom. Individuals investing directly (eschewing the financial wisdom of professionals) found the same conventional wisdom on the websites of the investment firms who catered to them, including Charles Schwab, Fidelity, and TD Ameritrade.

All followers of this "wisdom" believe in the same principles.

- "Asset allocation" based upon Modern Portfolio Theory is the preferred method to diversify and meet goals.

- Rebalancing your portfolio on a regular basis is mandatory. This means taking additional risk by selling bonds and buying stocks when stocks drop in price.

- Investments should always be held for the long-term. This means never selling in a declining stock market because "stocks make 10%-12% over the long run" and will eventually revert to an arbitrary mean/average return. [Note well: The 10% or greater return assumption is absolutely not true for several reasons discussed later in this book.]

- Diversification of equity (stock) investments into various categories significantly reduces downside correlation between asset classes and therefore reduces the risk of principal loss.

What the disciples of the "conventional wisdom" did not tell you or did not know—

- There are other prudent strategies besides "asset allocation" to diversify risk and meet specific financial needs.

- There are ways to modify portfolios without taking more risk (rebalancing) when the equity markets drop.

- Almost all institutions and financial advisors give out "cookie cutter advice" because of legal and business-related reasons.

- The 40 years of financial leverage leading up to the crash of 2008 artificially inflated the value of almost all asset classes, making historical returns not meaningful for predicting future returns.

When the bubble of inflated asset prices burst, there were no meaningful non-leveraged "average," "mean" or "normalized" values for many assets. Without non-leveraged values, it is difficult to determine with certainty what many assets, including your home, are truly worth! Not knowing the value of your investments is disconcerting and frightening. Even scarier are the underlying assumptions made to promote the "conventional wisdom" used to manage your current investments.

No theory of any kind works without first making specific assumptions. Theories are not facts, and without assumptions theories cannot "work."

Some of the underlying assumptions of the asset allocation models based upon Modern Portfolio Theory are:

1. Investors have unlimited time horizons.

2. The measurement of risk (*Beta* or β) in asset classes is stable from one time period to the next.

3. Rebalancing (buying riskier, poorly performing assets at the expense of selling better performing ones) is necessary.

4. Asset values will return to their mean/average valuations over time.

5. Investors are "rational" and risk adverse. They are not emotional.

6. Politics and investor psychology have no effect on the markets.

None of these assumptions held in 2008, meaning the investment advice you received was and is wrong! Absolutely and positively wrong. So why are financial advisors continuing to spew out advice based on this outdated "conventional wisdom?"

There are several important reasons why many financial advisors are still recommending "asset allocation" and "holding stocks for the long run."

1) Many advisors are unaware of alternative strategies for managing your money. They were never taught a different way to protect and invest your assets. Most financial advisors, including those who are CERTIFIED FINANCIAL PLANNER™ practitioners, are primarily trained in financial planning and not in the fields of investment analysis, investment strategy, or life insurance. Without this training or experience, they may not have the tools necessary to design and tailor customized investment strategies from scratch.

2) The recommendation of alternative strategies may not be as lucrative for advisors and their firms. Most advisors are paid

by having assets (your money) under management. The advisor earns a fee or commission on your assets every year—typically 1%—whether or not changes are made in your portfolio. The use of other strategies, such as holding a higher percentage of risk-free or guaranteed assets in your portfolio, may result in less income to the advisors and their firms. No wonder many advisors tell their clients to "hold on" to "risky" assets like stocks and bonds!

3) The financial industry's traditional methodology for monitoring and measuring the performance of your account is not based upon the *actual* performance of your account. Generally, advisors judge themselves based on how well your account performs relative to various market indices or benchmarks. The performance of your "asset allocation" account is usually expressed in *relative* terms ("You should be happy because you lost less than the S&P 500!") and not in *absolute* terms ("You should feel miserable because you lost money."). I believe expressing performance in *relative* terms is wrong because investors like you are probably more interested in *absolute* returns, similar to the way Will Rogers was more concerned with the *return of* his money rather than the *return on* his money. Losing your money is painful even if you lost less than an arbitrary index!

4) Wealth management firms do not want to look foolish, since they have collectively raised several trillion dollars by telling clients that "asset allocation" based upon Modern Portfolio Theory works! Firms that tell clients to stay with their "asset allocation" continue to collect lucrative fees on the money they keep under management. For example, Bank of America's (including Merrill Lynch) head of global wealth management, Sallie Krawcheck, is a supporter of asset allocation. In the October 5, 2009, issue of *Barron's*, Ms. Krawcheck was quoted as saying, "While some of the old lessons were battered a bit in 2008, they still hold true: There is only one free lunch in investing, and this is asset allocation. Over time, it consistently leads to higher returns

and lower risk." Interestingly, in the same issue of *Barron's*, Mark Taborsky, executive vice president for asset allocation at Pacific Investment Management Company (PIMCO), expressed the opposite opinion, and warned of the shortcomings of the traditional approach to asset allocation. He argued that we are in a "new normal" and "that's why relying on history is dangerous." Not surprisingly, Krawcheck's firm earns lucrative fees when her brokers (called financial advisors at Merrill Lynch) manage client assets using an asset allocation model.

Traditional asset allocation has failed miserably since 2000. Yet, it remains the "conventional wisdom" of financial advisors for the reasons mentioned above. **I believe you deserve a better way to diversify and invest your assets in our "new normal" economic environment.**

The "better way" to manage your investments, discussed in greater detail in later chapters, is a multi-tiered approach that focuses on your unique objectives and risk tolerance. How does my recommended approach differ from the conventional wisdom? Most of the underlying assumptions are the opposite of those in the traditional asset allocation models still being used by many investment firms and advisors to manage money. The other differences are related to how and why your assets are organized and managed using this method. Rather than placing all your assets in one portfolio, investments are layered into multiple portfolios tailored to your varying needs.

The "new" assumptions are:

1. Investors are concerned with actual returns and not relative returns.

2. Investors do not live forever, and therefore, do not have unlimited time horizons.

3. Investors are concerned with taxes related to their investments.

4. The measurement of investor risk aversion is complex and cannot be adequately measured by a one-page questionnaire designed as a portal into an asset allocation model.

5. Investors are emotional about their money and may not be rational when faced with large portfolio gains or losses. The pain most investors feel from portfolio losses is greater than the joy they receive from portfolio gains.

6. Most individual investors define their appropriate portfolio risk as "being able to sleep at night" and not in mathematical terms.

Most followers of conventional asset allocation lump investments into one giant pot based on "cookie-cutter" objectives. I recommend creating several distinct portfolios, each with separate risk and return requirements. The simplest version of this approach organizes or layers investments into three broad categories:

1. **Basic Needs:** The assets you need to live and survive on a day-to-day basis, including emergencies.

2. **Wants, Wishes & Desires:** The assets you need to do the things you want, wish, or desire to do (your "non-basic" needs).

3. **Legacy:** The assets you want to gift, give away, or distribute to others, during your lifetime or after your death (your estate and gift planning).

The first category, **Basic Needs,** is all about investing in a way that allows you to sleep well at night, every night. Regardless of domestic or worldwide events, you will sleep peacefully because the investments you own are guaranteed to provide you with the income you need to live on a day-to-day basis.

The second category, **Wants, Wishes & Desires,** involves diversification and the prudent management of risk given the return you desire. This may include asset allocation, but is more likely to involve a strategy of asset-liability matching and/or portfolio insurance to limit the potential loss of your investments.

Note: Many financial advisors are not equipped to provide competent advice for anything other than asset allocation.

The last category, **Legacy**, refers to your estate plan, which can include philanthropic planning and charitable giving. Estate planning (wills, trusts and related documents) ensures that your financial goals and wishes are met during your lifetime, in the event of your incapacity, and after your death. This type of planning can be as simple or as complicated as you desire, depending upon your net worth, personal objectives, and legal and tax considerations.

This represents part of my framework for a multi-tiered approach to managing your money. To meet your changing needs and goals over time, this framework takes many factors into consideration, including your objectives, net worth, types of assets, and estate plan. Additional categories and layers may be integrated into the framework as necessary to address your varying needs, goals and time horizons. The investment strategies, designed for each category or layer, are a function of these and other variables including your risk tolerance and return expectations.

In the conventional wisdom approach to asset allocation, you "fill in the boxes" of a standardized investment policy statement based on "cookie cutter" objectives, "throw" all your funds into the suggested computerized asset allocation model that uses predetermined asset classes, and then, "hope" the advisor (and/or the advisor's firm) you are working with is adept at choosing investment managers.

The multi-tiered framework I recommend is much different—it is the foundation of a truly customized, comprehensive method for managing your money. This integrated approach requires a level of expertise that many advisors are not currently equipped to provide. It can only be accomplished by people who are knowledgeable and skillful in the areas of financial planning, estate planning, and investment analysis and management.

In the multi-tiered approach, investment strategies are tailored to each category or layer of assets. This means the custom investment policy and asset mix used to provide your "Basic Needs" may be completely different from what is used for your "Wants, Wishes & Desires." For many people, shifting from the "conventional wisdom" to my multi-layered approach increases the amount of guaranteed assets purchased for their "Basic Needs" category. This should lower the fees paid to advisors for ongoing investment advice since it is difficult for advice-givers to justify charging 1% or more for managing guaranteed investments.

Traditional asset allocation based on Modern Portfolio Theory has not met investor expectations for over a decade, and is unlikely to work well in the future. It needs to be replaced with a better approach to managing your money. I highly recommend the multi-tiered investment approach because it provides a better method for matching investments to an investor's risk profile, and it is more likely to produce positive returns.

Bottom Line: The multi-tiered investment approach is superior to the "conventional wisdom" (traditional asset allocation) model for the following reasons:

- More effectively matches investment strategies to an investor's risk profile and objectives.

- More likely to produce positive returns.

- Potentially less expensive – ongoing investment management fees may be less in the long run.

CHAPTER 2

A BRIEF HISTORY OF FINANCIAL ADVICE AND THE RISE OF ASSET ALLOCATION
How We Got Into This Asset Allocation Mess and What Went So Terribly Wrong in 2008

Most people love money. Money may not buy happiness, but having enough of it does make life easier. Because most of us do not live off the land, we use money to purchase the goods and services we need to survive and thrive. More money allows us to live better, to prosper, and to have a comfortable margin of safety. Most people want to make their money grow, but they are not financial experts. They have to look elsewhere for financial advice.

Before the Great Depression, the financial advisory business operated very differently from how it does today. There were fewer people giving advice and most of the advice went to the wealthy with excess capital to invest. Some of the same institutional names in the news today were giving advice back then: Brown Brothers Harriman, Goldman Sachs, J.P. Morgan, Merrill Lynch, etc. These firms were headed by strong individuals with a sense of purpose. They enjoyed making money for themselves, and they attempted to help their clients through quality research and prudent advice.

The way advice was given before the Great Depression changed little after that event. A "customer's man" working for a broker or dealer took orders and made suggestions to clients. The typical customer's man came from a wealthy family and had connections to other wealthy individuals and families. He did not cold call, seek clients through seminars, or write newsletters. He eschewed those activities in favor of the more socially correct methods of gaining clients: social connections and referrals. The customer's man simply let people know he was in the business and waited for the orders to come his way.

After World War II, some important changes occurred. The United States recovered from the Great Depression and experienced powerful economic growth. American business was on a roll, and factories burst into full swing. Additional factories were built to handle increased manufacturing demand. During the Eisenhower administration, roads and airports were built to quickly transport goods and people anywhere in the country. A housing boom developed and people began moving to the suburbs. Employment rates rose and the general wealth of the nation began to increase on a sustained basis.

The customer's man was still giving investment advice, but a new salesman/advice-giver came onto the scene: the stockbroker. Yes, the customer's man was technically a broker of stocks with loyalty to his broker/dealer. But the customer's man did not aggressively look for new accounts, and he certainly did not cultivate relationships with the average citizen. The stockbroker did, and the dream of Charlie Merrill (of the famed Merrill Lynch) to "bring Wall Street to Main Street" came true.

Stockbrokers, primarily men until Muriel Siebert, actively looked for business on a commission basis. Brokers' earnings (commissions) were based on transactions (trades of stocks, bonds and other securities) executed for clients. In the post-war era, it was very expensive to buy and sell stocks, bonds and mutual funds. Stock and bond trades could cost 4% of the market value of the underlying security. The average cost to purchase a mutual fund was 7%. Brokers who transacted lots of business were considered "successful" by their firms. This commission structure enabled many brokers to become wildly successful—as wealthy as their best clients.

In 1975, one year after what was then the worst decline in stocks since the Great Depression, fixed income commissions charged by brokers were deregulated and allowed to float. The investment industry initially fought hard against deregulation, claiming it would ruin the business. Surprisingly, deregulation did not ruin anyone's business. The baby boom generation was coming of age and entering the work force. Boomers began saving their money in pension plans. The pension fund managers had to invest that money somewhere, and much of it was invested in financial assets. Corporate profits grew, and some of that money was invested in equities. The business of Wall Street grew dramatically after the deregulation of 1975. The investment industry did not die after deregulation—it flourished.

After 1975, stockbrokers continued to do what they did best: earn commissions by selling their firm's investment ideas and products. The stockbroker's typical approach was to cold-call potential clients, usually wealthy individuals, present a stock or bond idea, and ask for an order. If successful, the stockbroker nurtured the relationship to gain the investor's confidence. This increased the broker's chances of investing more of that client's money and earning additional commissions.

From a regulatory perspective, this transaction-oriented, commission-based stockbroker business model was a legal disaster waiting to happen. The three major problems were:

1. The best interests of the clients were not necessarily served. In a transaction-oriented business, many brokers focused on earning commissions rather than providing comprehensive financial advice.

2. There were no incentives or it was not practical for stockbrokers to provide comprehensive financial planning to their clients. Even though many brokerage firms had financial planning, insurance and trust capabilities, many stockbrokers were reluctant to work with those departments. There were no financial incentives for the brokers to do so and many found the process too onerous. Also, stockbrokers were concerned that the representatives from those areas would hurt the broker's client relationships or "steal" their clients.

3. It created too many compliance issues and legal problems. It was a nightmare for the legal and compliance departments of broker/dealers to monitor brokers and the investment advice given to clients. With over 100,000 representatives nationwide giving out almost as many investment ideas, it was logistically impossible to keep tabs on the suitability of the investment advice given to every customer.

After the late 1970's, wirehouses (stock brokerage firms) expanded, and new firms and financial advice-givers emerged in the marketplace. "Discount brokerages" (do-it-yourself investing for individual investors) and "financial planning" broker/dealers (catering to "independent advisors") were born. The discount brokerages provided a place for individuals to do their own trades without an advisor. The financial planning broker/dealers specialized in providing services to independent advisors or financial planners who were not required to exclusively sell the firm's proprietary products and research.

Many of the early independent advisors started their careers as captive insurance agents who grew tired of the "life insurance is the answer to every financial need" mantra of their employers. They began providing comprehensive financial solutions to their clients, coined the phrase "financial planning," and called themselves "financial planners." These independent advisors—financial planners—formed their own associations (e.g., The International Association for Financial Planning), developed their own standards (e.g., the CERTIFIED FINANCIAL PLANNER™ certification), and offered a reasonable alternative to the commissioned stockbroker. The early financial planners understood insurance products and estate planning (at least from an insurance perspective). They primarily sold mutual funds instead of individual stocks and bonds, and generally looked out for the best interests of their clients.

The very wealthy, of course, had other options for managing their money: personal trust companies and family offices. Trust companies flourished, managing the assets of the rich and their families. The trust companies offered services that included trust and estate administration, investment management, generational planning, philanthropic planning and charitable giving, bill-paying, and financial counseling. Some wealthy families arranged for private management of their finances and investments across generations by establishing family offices. Some successful family offices expanded into multi-family offices providing financial management and other services to the founding family as well as other wealthy families.

Until the early 1980's, broker/dealers for stockbrokers and financial planners shared a very big problem: the advice given to clients with similar investment needs was not standardized. This lack of standardization made it easier to sue the broker/dealers for giving improper advice to clients. For example, a client could go to a dozen different advisors working for the same firm and get twelve substantially different investment solutions. This potential exposure to legal liability was of great concern to the compliance officers and legal counsel of wirehouses and financial planning broker/dealers.

Many trust companies already had a solution to the problem. They standardized the management of investment accounts by using asset allocation based upon Modern Portfolio Theory (MPT). At that time, MPT was considered a newer method of managing money.

Asset allocation is defined as the diversification of money among various predetermined asset classes. Modern Portfolio Theory (MPT) is a mathematical model of finance that attempts to maximize portfolio returns and minimize risk through the precise diversification into various asset classes. MPT relies on historical values and presumes several things including returns will eventually revert to their averages. In other words, the price of "risky" assets like stocks and bonds will revert to their average or "mean value" in the long run. I believe the reliance upon MPT's approach to asset allocation is the reason so much money was lost by so many in October 2008!

The history of asset allocation is filled with theories from scholars, some of whom became Nobel laureates. The genesis of asset allocation can be traced to Harry Markowitz's pioneering work during the early 1950's in the area of risk and investing. While at the University of Chicago, Markowitz studied the available research regarding stock prices. At that time, the analysis focused on determining the present value of investments without considering the impact of risk to return. He theorized that investors diversify their portfolios because they are concerned with risk as well as return. Investors traditionally accomplished this by finding individual stocks or other securities with attractive risk-reward characteristics and combining them into a portfolio. He thought that a better method for creating portfolios was to select securities based upon the total risk-return impact to the overall portfolio, and not just the individual risk and return of each security. Therefore, from a risk-return perspective, it was important to analyze how securities performed in concert with each other within a given portfolio.

Markowitz defined portfolio risk as variance because, in the pre-calculator world of slide rules, it was easier to calculate than semi-variance (downside risk). He theorized that risk could be reduced by combining assets with different co-variances, thereby creating an "efficient" portfolio. Therefore, portfolio risk could be decreased by adding risky assets (stocks and bonds) to a portfolio, provided the assets were not perfectly correlated with each other. In simple terms, some risky assets with positive expected returns "zig" while other ones "zag," smoothing out returns by reducing volatility. When a portfolio is "efficient," additional diversification does not reduce portfolio risk for a given expected return. Markowitz published his theory in an article called "Portfolio Selection" in *The Journal of Finance* in 1952, while working at the RAND Corporation. Eventually, others read his theory, and it became a revolutionary investment topic. In 1990, Harry Markowitz, Merton H. Miller and William F. Sharpe were awarded the Nobel Prize for Economics for their pioneering work in this field of study.

Markowitz faced a problem early in his research. His theory made sense on paper, but making it work in the real world was impractical at that time. Given that there were tens of thousands of securities traded in the markets every day, how could various portfolios with optimal mixes of securities be designed to put his theory into practice?

In 1958, James Tobin helped turn theory into reality by adding a risk-free asset (Treasuries) to Markowitz's analysis, allowing for leverage. In 1959, Markowitz added to his earlier work and published a book called *Portfolio Selection: Efficient Diversification of Investments*.

William F. Sharpe built on this research and was one of the originators of the Capital Asset Pricing Model (CAPM). His 1964 paper on "Capital Asset Prices: A Theory of Market Equilibrium Under Conditions of Risk" was published in *The Journal of Finance*. Sharpe's paper described CAPM and defined the notion of market and individual security risk (systemic and specific security risk). Sharpe believed the specific risk of individual securities could be diversified away by owning a basket of the securities (later to become market indexes), assuming markets are "efficient." He concluded that a portfolio's excess return beyond a relevant benchmark came from its risk. More risk, therefore, equated to a higher expected return. This made it easier to construct an "efficient" portfolio. Around the same time, the idea of CAPM was independently developed by John Lintner and Jack Treynor.

In 1958, Franco Modigliani and Merton Miller proposed a theorem on the optimal capital structure of a corporation which became known as the "Modigliani-Miller Theorem." They believed, under certain assumptions, that the market valuation of a company is not affected by how it is capitalized (equity, debt, or both) or its dividend policy.

The collective works of all of these individuals set the stage for the birth of the indexing industry in 1973, which eventually made asset allocation practical. Using indexes in lieu of individual investments made it easier and more affordable to buy and trade baskets of securities (e.g., S&P 500) of the asset classes necessary to build an "efficient" portfolio. Because of indexing, asset allocation caught on in popularity in the industry. Asset allocation based upon Modern Portfolio Theory is currently the most widely used method of managing a total portfolio of risky assets for institutions and individuals. Today, many, if not most, corporate and individual investors' assets are invested and managed with the help of a computerized asset allocation model.

Most trust companies eagerly embraced asset allocation because, in theory, it enabled investment managers to construct individual portfolios that produced returns commensurate with each client's objectives and desired level of risk. Also, since trust companies earn fees based on assets under management, asset allocation provided a more profitable way to manage accounts. This strategy made perfect sense, assuming the risk and return assumptions used in the asset allocation models reflected reality.

Asset allocation became the perfect answer in the late 1980's for broker/dealer compliance officers who sought consistency in the advice registered representatives gave to clients. An asset allocation model meant all financial advisors (working for a particular broker/dealer) used similar cookie-cutter investment strategies, lessening the chance of lawsuits. Most compliance departments required advisors to use an investment policy statement (IPS) with their firm's asset allocation models. The IPS was primarily used as a conduit into the firm's asset allocation product, though, it did help quantify the general risk and return requirements of each client.

Asset allocation also became the preferred answer for financial advisors and intermediaries who sought to manage all of their clients' assets in a highly organized and rational way. Eventually, the wirehouses promoted this idea through a change in their representative compensation structure. Financial advisors found they could earn significantly more money simply by placing all of their clients' money into an asset allocation product and charging a 1% (or more) advisory fee on the assets under management. An advisor with $100 million under management who bought into asset allocation could earn $1 million or more per year in fees!

Things began to change as the entire financial industry jumped on the "asset allocation" bandwagon. Direct marketers (Fidelity, Schwab, Waterhouse, Ameritrade, etc.), wirehouses, individual planners, and even insurance agents began using asset allocation models. Investment management firms created new products, both mutual fund and separately managed accounts, to "fit" into the investment categories of the asset allocation models used for their clients. "Fee-based" planning became the business model of choice, with most wirehouses and individual advisors charging a yearly fee (usually 1% of the market value of assets held) to "manage" a client's portfolio using asset allocation, rather than taking commissions on individual securities transactions. Assets flowed into the burgeoning indexing industry from those who believed that active management was too risky.

Almost all the firms using asset allocation models assumed that each asset class would revert to its mean (average) return over time. Unfortunately, this assumption proved incorrect. Since 2000, this reliance upon the wrong assumptions has led to many disappointed investors.

The 1975 deregulation of commissions on fixed income securities sparked investment growth, but 1999 marked the year of explosive growth in Wall Street banking and derivative activity. Derivatives are securities that are valued based upon the price of another underlying security, commodity, or event. Interestingly, many of our current economic problems can be traced to 1999, when Congress removed the barriers that prevented commercial banks from entering the investment industry. Prior to 1999, commercial banking and investment banking activities were separated in accordance with the second Glass-Steagall Act (the Banking Act of 1933). This Act was passed on June 16, 1933, in response to a high proportion of commercial bank failures in early 1933.

After 1999, banks, and insurance companies such as American International Group, Inc. (AIG), began paying Wall Street wages and bonuses to executives who helped those financial institutions greatly leverage their asset bases in the name of earnings growth. This additional leverage helped keep the financial bubble growing until it collapsed in 2008.

The problem with today's financial advice-givers (including the advisors selling books on TV, radio personalities, direct sellers, stockbrokers, fee-only planners, insurance agents, and others) is not their lack of desire to serve you. I find most advisors really do care about their clients. The problem is not their lack of expertise or knowledge in a specific area. Most are book smart or have experts they can call upon. And it is not their lack of ability to access financial products. Quality financial products are avail-able almost everywhere these days. The problem is your advisor believed (and probably still believes) in the pre-bubble risk and return assumptions that are still being used in asset allocation models today. As we shall see in the next chapter, those assump-tions are very, very wrong.

CHAPTER 3

THE 10% RETURN AND EQUALIZATION LIES

The traditional investment advice given by the financial industry is based on the following assumptions:

- Stocks earn, on average, 10%-12% per year.
- Stocks will revert to a "mean" value in the long run (equalization).
- Asset allocation diversifies your assets and significantly minimizes your investment risk.

This advice proved to be flat-out wrong but it is still accepted as the "conventional wisdom" in the industry. Millions of individuals invested their money based on these "lies," and during the latter part of 2008, they lost a significant portion of their net worth.

The 10% Return Assumption "Lie"

The 10% equity return number is routinely assumed in the asset allocation models used by the entire financial industry. You see 10% equity returns assumed by many trust companies, stock brokerages, direct sellers of financial services, and insurance companies selling variable life insurance products.

The 10% number comes from the interpretation of several Eugene Fama and Kenneth French scholarly studies analyzing domestic stock returns. During the time periods studied by Fama and French, stocks did indeed return better than 10%, but the people and firms promoting the study often tend to omit several vitally important facts:

- The price/earnings (P/E) multiple paid by investors for stocks (risky assets) more than doubled during the 1928-2000 time period, and increased nearly 8 times from its low in the early 1930's!

- The dividends paid to stockholders shrank from 4.45% to 1.16% during the same time period.

- The United States saw asset prices grow at their "historic" rates (10% on average) because of 40 years of financial leverage. To assume stocks will continue growing by 10%-12% per year, one must assume that earnings will be strong enough to drive P/E ratios permanently higher. This is highly unlikely in the current economic environment of financial deleveraging!

Stocks did return more than 9.5% per year during nine separate 20-year time periods (starting at January 1) from 1942 to 2008. In each one of these periods the P/E ratio for the market at least doubled! This means stocks are more likely to give double-digit returns when they start from a low P/E base. If this remains true, double-digit returns will not come again unless stocks either crash further to single-digit P/E ratios (e.g., a DOW of 5,500) or do nothing for a long period of time when earnings "catch up" to current prices. Either way, this does not portend consistent double-digit returns over the long haul for most people who invested before 2009.

I believe most domestic stocks are highly unlikely to return 10% per year going forward from current levels for another reason:

earnings growth. Growth in earnings, the dividend yield, and changes in valuations (changes in P/E ratios) are the three components of stock market return. The economic environment we are entering is likely one of a deflationary process rather than inflation. The private sector (people like you and me) has recently started to save now that home values and investments (held in risky assets) have deteriorated. More savings means less spending, and that foreshadows less growth in domestic corporate earnings.

There is also a sound pragmatic argument as to why stocks cannot return over 10% in the long run. The argument against stocks returning 10% per year was presented by Peter Bernstein in an article he wrote in 2000 for *Financial Analysts Journal,* and it goes something like this: If you had invested $10,000 in the year of George Washington's inauguration, and earned 10% compounded interest (annually with no withdrawals), then you would end up today with more than 2/3 the GDP of the USA and more than the GDP of both China and Japan. It should be obvious from this example that no one can become that rich; therefore, nothing can compound at 10% forever! This pragmatic argument explains in part why most of the great investors of the past several decades (George Soros, Paul Tudor Jones, Michael Steinhart, and others) either quit their games or routinely gave away their money as they made it.

But the pragmatic argument did not kill stocks and other investments in October 2008. It was the massive "deleveraging" that proved the pragmatic argument prophetic. It turns out the amount of leverage (borrowing to make investments) in the system was not in the billions of dollars or hundreds of billions of dollars. It was in the tens of trillions of dollars! This amount, combined with the guarantees made through derivative investments necessary to carry the leverage, surprised even the most seasoned Wall Street observers.

The current deleveraging will not end quickly because the

amount of the leverage is too large. Equities probably reached their bottom valuations in March 2009, but where will they go from 2010 levels? I believe equities will still be valued in traditional ways, primarily by discounting future earnings streams. P/E ratios investors pay for these securities will reflect the less leveraged and greater savings-oriented world we now live in. And this portends stocks growing at a rate that is far less than 10%.

The 10% return assumption used by the financial industry (for equities) came about during a time period that ended with the bursting of a "once in a lifetime" financial bubble. I believe it is time to stop using the ridiculous 10% estimate for projections and instead use a more reasonable estimate. Yet many financial advisors are still relying upon the outdated "conventional wisdom" that gives clients a false sense of hope.

Stocks Revert to their Mean Value in the Long Run—The Equalization "Lie"

The first lie, the 10% return assumption, is based on another lie—the belief that all stocks will eventually revert to a normalized value, also defined as a mean or average value. This value is a mean price determined by mathematical analysis of years of reported historical data. In theory, an overvalued asset will go down (or not go up) until its average valuation is reached. Conversely, an undervalued asset will rise (or not go down with other assets) until it reaches its "fair" market value (mean value). The flaw in this thinking is that, in our new world of deleveraging, a fair market value for many assets is now in question!

The financial leverage that expanded the prices of assets for over 40 years is now unwinding. This lack of future leverage will change the fair market values of all financial assets for the rest of our lives. A home worth $500,000 five years ago may be worth only $300,000 today, and perhaps less tomorrow. Stocks that previously sold at 20 times their estimated earnings may sell for much lower multiples in the future. Bonds that are now at historically low yields are expected to lose money when interest rates rise again. The inability to place a reasonable estimated market value on many assets further compounds the problem. Without the past leverage in our financial system, we simply cannot determine with certainty what many assets are really worth today!

Asset Allocation Diversifies Assets and Significantly Minimizes Investment Risk—The Diversification "Lie"

In the aftermath of the market collapse, what are you supposed to do with your assets? Some investment advisors and ardent supporters of asset allocation continue to recommend "holding on" to your failed stocks and bonds as the best solution over the long-term. But if the "normalized" values for these securities will be less in the future because of financial deleveraging, when will the value of your portfolio come back, how long will it take to make-up the losses, and at what point is it safe to invest? How can asset allocation make sense if the "normalized" values cannot be determined with certainty? How can you safely invest using a theory which assumes prices of risky assets (stocks and bonds) will revert to their mean or normalized values when you do not know how to determine the normalized value for each asset?

All theories, including "asset allocation," are based on certain assumptions holding true. Some of the assumptions made by investment advisors who are proponents of asset allocation are:

1. Investors have unlimited time horizons.

2. Investors are "rational" and not emotional.

3. *Beta* (β), or the risk associated with the asset classes, is stable and easily quantified.

4. Rebalancing is necessary to maintain targeted portfolio risk and returns.

5. Asset prices will always revert to a "mean" value based on historical prices.

None of these assumptions held in the crash of 2008. The financial pundits seemed to be blindsided by the unprecedented turn of events in our economy and many financial experts are still trying to figure out what went so wrong and why. An examination of the five basic assumptions underlying most asset allocation models can help us understand what happened when the market collapsed.

Assumptions 1 & 2: Investors have unlimited time horizons and are rational (not emotional) when making investment decisions.

No sane person can agree with these first two assumptions, given that we will not live forever, and emotions do play a role in how we invest. Unlike some institutions, individual investors will eventually die. Therefore, individuals must have limited—not unlimited—time horizons. These investors, particularly retirees, may not have enough time to recoup a large loss. Also, individual investors are not "rational" or unemotional when it comes to their money. Most people are not immune to market fluctuations and have a hard time passively watching their net worth decline. How can you sleep at night knowing that your investment strategy will not protect you in an unforeseen financial disaster? For most people, the emotional or psychic pain associated with the loss of wealth is greater than the enjoyment that comes from gaining it. Unlike "rational" institutions, individual investors find it difficult to readily stick with an investment strategy that has lost money. An institution experiences less pain from losing money because it expects to have a steady stream of new assets coming in the door. Institutions also have longer or unlimited time horizons enabling them to wait for investments to recover.

Assumption 3: Beta (β), the measurement of risk of a portfolio relative to the overall market, is stable and easily quantified.

This third assumption did not hold because the volatility of stocks, bonds and other assets significantly increased in late 2008, and *Beta* (β) could not be accurately measured using historical data. The concept that the volatility of a portfolio could be measured by its *Beta* (β) did not hold when the market collapsed. In other words, *Beta* (β) was not a good predictor of the riskiness of a portfolio in a crash.

Assumption 4: Rebalancing is necessary to maintain targeted portfolio risk and return.

Paradoxically, this fourth assumption resulted in the opposite of what investors desired or expected during the crash. Rebalancing of portfolios is one of the ways financial advisors justify charging a 1% fee. In theory, rebalancing is supposed to maximize upside participation in a rising market by maintaining an optimal portfolio mix based on stated investment objectives and risk/return expectations. Instead, rebalancing resulted in exposing a portfolio to more risk in a declining market. Most investors want to take less risk when their assets are declining in order to prevent a change in their lifestyle. Taking more risk when assets decline is counterintuitive.

Assumption 5: In the long run, the price of an asset will revert to its mean value, based on historical prices.

This assumption did not hold because of the financial leverage in the economic system. There were no mean or average values for many investments to revert to since the "normalized" values changed because of financial leverage.

Many advisors did their best to help investors by using this conventional diversification and investment tool called "asset allocation." Unfortunately, many of the assumptions behind that tool were misguided or wrong. The high net worth investing client deserves better from his or her advisors today!

Where will equity prices go from here? I have no idea! In the long run, most stocks should rise from the lows of the post-2008 market because the future will eventually be brighter for earnings, even if earnings rise at a lower rate than in previous decades. As usual, history repeated itself. Well before earnings actually improved, the market started rising when there was "light at the end of the tunnel," or in the words of Federal Reserve Chairman Ben S. Bernanke, "green shoots" of economic recovery.

Those who were lucky or smart enough to invest for the first time at the market bottom, wherever it may be, will see spectacular returns that are far greater than 10%. Those who invested before the crash of 2008, or after we came off the bottom, will not see future returns greater than 10% because the growth in earnings will not justify those returns. History suggests that the rebounds off our lows will be more volatile as will further market "corrections."

The 10%-12% equity return assumption used by many advisors was wrong in the past and will probably be wrong in the future. The concept of assets returning to historical "normalized" values is difficult to comprehend when those average values came from a time characterized by substantial financial leverage, whereas now we are living in a time of deleverage. Investors will be better served by using their own, more conservative return assumptions, far less than history would suggest.

Asset allocation and diversification techniques still have a place in many portfolios but should not be relied upon as your sole investment strategy. The old models and assumptions must be reassessed and fine-tuned to reflect your personal objectives and the global economy, today and in the future. While the money you lost because of the "lies" or faulty reasoning inherent in the conventional wisdom of the financial industry cannot be replaced, there is a better way to defensively manage your assets as you navigate your way through the unchartered waters that is now our economic environment.

CHAPTER 4

A BETTER AND LESS EXPENSIVE WAY TO MANAGE YOUR ASSETS

The cover of this book promises a better way to invest your money, one that will allow you to sleep at night and provide you with reasonable returns. A better method does exist and I believe you should be using it.

Most of us believe diversification, or "not putting all of your eggs in one basket," is wise. I do too, unless your goal is to increase your net worth quickly at the expense of safety. We now know "asset allocation"—at least how it is used by most people in the financial services industry—did not work during the financial crisis of 2008. We also know the 10% equity return assumption is false, as is the assumption that stocks return to a previously determined "mean" value. So if asset allocation alone does not work, how should we prudently diversify and find an investment strategy that works? The answer is a multi-tiered or multi-layered investment framework that enables you to invest wisely and sleep well at night. This approach is based on the following five parameters discussed in greater detail below:

1. Determine who you are—the "who behind you."

2. "Layer" your investments.

3. Develop a written plan for your customized strategy.

4. Determine the proper investments for your strategy, given current and future market conditions.

5. Monitor and adjust your strategy when necessary.

First, determine who you are. Really! The *who behind you* will help you determine how to diversify and invest. [Note: This assumes you will not invest like most people and dump all your money into an asset allocation model.] There are many psychology-based guides, books, and articles to help you discover who you truly are or the "who behind you." An important part of this process is understanding your relationship with money, and why and how you make investment decisions. One of the best guides I have found comes from research and surveys conducted by Russ Alan Prince and Karen Maru File. Through their extensive research, funded by *Institutional Investor Magazine* over a decade ago, Prince and File identified and profiled nine unique high net worth personality types. Each personality type accurately (at least in my opinion) describes how investors think about money, risk, legacy planning, etc. Another chapter of this book will examine this framework of investor personalities and psychologies in greater detail.

For example, a **"Family Steward"** is most concerned with leaving wealth intact to his or her spouse, other family members, and charities, in that order. A Family Steward will gladly "leave some money on the table" if it means knowing the family's wealth is safe. Many Family Stewards thought asset allocation was "safe," but now know better!

An **"Innovator"** simply needs money to seek out or create new opportunities. Innovators feel that money is not to be kept, but invested (or given away if they are charitably minded) in a way that uses new ideas or technology to improve their financial situation (or that of their charities). Innovators rarely invest for the very long-term since there are always new ideas and adventures to fund with their wealth.

These are just brief examples of two of the nine personalities Prince and File identified. The "who behind you" may fit within one of these nine personalities or may be a combination of several of these personalities. In any case, finding out how you think about money can be a revelation. I have seen couples cry with tears of joy after discovering why they argue constantly about money—they have different "investor" personalities.

There are, of course, several other constructive ways to determine the financial "who behind you" and they should also be explored. It is absolutely vital that you know who you are before determining: (1) How to invest your money; and (2) How much of your assets to place in each of the investment categories described in the next section.

Once you know your financial self, the "who behind you," your next steps are to: layer your assets in defined categories; develop a written plan with your customized strategy; choose investments to fit your strategy; and, monitor and adjust your plan over time.

It is crucial to "layer" your assets into separate categories for investment purposes. This is much easier to do after you have determined the "who behind you." Then you can develop a customized, written plan that covers your goals and strategies for all layers of your assets. An integral part of your plan is to determine the appropriate investments for each layer and to have a mechanism in place to monitor and adjust your plan as necessary (in response to changes in your personal life, market conditions, and the economy).

For some people, particularly those with complex or large estates, there may be several "layers" and categories to consider. For most individuals and retirees, there will be only three categories, so that is what I will use as an example:

- **Basic Needs:** What you need to survive.

- **Wants, Wishes & Desires:** The things you like or want to do, not including your basic needs and necessities.

- **Legacy:** What you want to give away during your lifetime and beyond; your estate plan.

Basic Needs

The first layer consists of the assets you need to sleep well at night, and I call it the "basic needs" or "what you need to survive" category. For some people with "enough" money, this is everything they have since they need all their assets guaranteed in order to sleep well at night! For others, this layer consists of a smaller part of their net worth because their needs are relatively modest or easily covered by their earned income, retirement income, and/or investment income. I define basic needs as all housing-related expenses, food, energy costs, medical expenses, insurance costs, emergency funds, and other necessities.

For example, Jim and Mary are a retired couple. After they estimated the income from their defined benefit retirement plan, IRAs, and social security, they calculated that they required another $28,000 per year to cover their basic needs and give them peace of mind. These needs should be covered through guaranteed and/or very safe investments. If the market crashes 10 years from now or the world goes into a depression, Jim and Mary will rest assured their basic needs will be met because their liabilities (the money they need) are matched to safe and/or guaranteed investments.

Jim and Mary can choose from many guaranteed and safe investments such as Treasuries (bills, notes, and zero coupon bonds), AAA-rated municipal securities, annuities issued from financially sound insurance companies, and "bulletproof" corporate bonds. Asset allocation and most risky individual investments have no place in the first category! Exceptions include rental real estate (where the rental income is predictable) and other assets acquired for asset-liability matching purposes (more on that later).

Wants, Wishes & Desires

The second layer of assets includes the things you like to do —your wants, wishes and desires that are not basic necessities. Some examples in this category include traveling, playing sports like tennis or golf (although some might put golf in the "basic need" category), and pursuing hobbies. Traveling the world and staying in five-star hotels are things most people would like to do, but they are certainly not basic necessities. The needs in this category can be met through asset-liability matching, asset allocation (assuming the asset allocation model is used correctly, i.e., programmed with the appropriate parameters for risk, return, social, economic, and political assumptions), or portfolio insurance strategies.

For example, assume Jim and Mary want to retire and take four vacations each year (including visiting their children who live out-of-state), purchase a new automobile every 4 years, eat out 3 days per week, spend $4,000 per year on clothing, and maintain a membership in their local country club. These things are important to them, but they could easily survive (basic needs) without getting to do all of them. Therefore, they should invest accordingly. They may need their assets to grow over time to meet their increasing obligations, which presumably will be higher each year due to modest inflation (I am assuming deflation—if any— will be short lived). Jim and Mary must prudently diversify and use a predetermined investment strategy designed to meet their desired and stated goals.

What should Jim and Mary take into consideration when selecting investment vehicles for their second layer? The "old" way of investing money, by simply using various investment managers or mutual funds in an arbitrary asset allocation model, is not appropriate in our current economic climate. A better way is to weigh several options (for every investment category) and choose those investments that make sense based on prevailing financial conditions. Some possibilities are open-end mutual funds, closed-end funds, separately managed accounts, and exchange traded funds.

An open-end mutual fund might make sense because of low fees and a large loss carry-forward that should eliminate future capital gains distributions for a number of years. A closed-end fund, with low fees selling at a substantial discount to net asset value (NAV), might offer a much higher yield and potential return (should the discount to NAV close over time). A separately managed account might use an investment manager favorable to Jim's and Mary's goals or needs. An exchanged traded fund might offer better and less expensive asset-liability matching characteristics.

The selection of the best investments for Jim and Mary should depend upon what is available at the time they choose to invest, and not upon their advisor's adherence to a single business model!

Legacy

The third layer of investments should be reserved exclusively for your legacy—the assets you want to give to others before and after you are gone. This is commonly known as "legacy planning" or estate planning and includes philanthropic planning and charitable giving. Legacy planning ensures that your money will be managed and distributed in accordance with your wishes, regardless of your net worth.

For example, Jim and Mary want to give away some of their money to charity today on a tax-advantaged basis and a portion of their estate to several charities after death. They want the majority of their estate to be divided fairly among their children from two marriages. They invest a portion of their assets to meet the financial requirements of the various trusts, insurance policies, and investment accounts set up to meet these needs.

The multi-layered approach to investing provides a high level of comfort because investors know that there is a "floor" to protect them during unfavorable markets (the first category-Basic Needs). This is very different from the typical asset allocation rebalancing that takes on more risk when the market drops. I believe most clients want to sleep at night and not take additional risk during bear markets!

The multi-layered approach is more difficult to effectively accomplish than the "asset allocation" approach. It forces you to figure out who you are (the psychological component) so that you can accurately focus on defining your basic "survival" needs, your pleasurable endeavors (the things you enjoy doing—not basic needs), and your legacy (estate planning and charitable giving goals). Then, it mandates the development of an investment policy—and custom investment policy statement—for each investment "layer." This approach also requires someone with the expertise to find suitable strategies and investments for each category. Finally, it requires coordination of all the "layers," including monitoring and adjusting over time, so that the overall plan makes sense for you and your family.

Some of the investment strategies might include asset allocation. Despite its flaw as an end-all strategy, asset allocation still has merit. Strategies could also include simple asset-liability matching, something most financial planners rarely use. For example, an investor can match his or her fuel costs (home, automobile, etc.) to energy investments bundled in an exchange traded fund designed to produce income. When the cost of energy rises, so will the income from the fund. Several other prudent strategies are also available. Investments should come from the total universe of what is currently available, and not be limited to mutual funds or what can be found in a separate account platform.

Regardless of the strategy, investors must diversify in more ways than ever before. We know from recent experience that the typical asset allocation did not protect us enough when equity markets collapsed. We also know that when fallen asset values rebound, they do so at differing speeds. Diversifying into domestic and foreign stocks, bonds, and real estate is not good enough anymore! Prudent investors must consider everything—stocks, bonds, mutual funds, commodities, real estate, art, collectibles, insurance, guaranteed investments, hedged investments, private equity and other investments—for inclusion in their asset mix. In my opinion, the average investor—not the one who wants to die with the most toys—cannot diversify enough!

The last part of the framework involves monitoring your investments and investment strategy on a regular basis. Your risk tolerance may change over time. Market valuations will fluctuate. Estate, income and investment tax laws will change too. Reviewing your situation on a regular basis is mandatory.

The beauty of this multi-tiered approach is that it works—every time. You know what your risk is in each layer (perhaps little or none in the first layer), and you can easily monitor your investment results. This approach also allows you to have a truly customized investment plan, something "asset allocation" promised but never accomplished.

A good financial advisor should be able to help you orchestrate this multi-tiered or multi-layered investment approach, but finding one who will is difficult. Almost all are stuck in the standard "asset allocation" rut, afraid to call clients with helpful information such as how and when to take tax losses. Almost all are reluctant to change their current business model which depends on acquiring assets under management using an asset allocation model. Also, most advisors do not have the knowledge or skill to write an investment policy statement from scratch, or to analyze investments for your benefit. Still, you should be able to find a competent professional to work with you.

CHAPTER 5

ARE STOCKS OVERVALUED AGAIN?

After stocks bottomed in March of 2009, they rallied over 55% by the following October to the delight of many. Price/Earnings (P/E) ratios jumped back to the mid-twenties. It appeared the United States crawled out of a long recession with the help of unprecedented fiscal stimulus, and advisors were again bold enough to pick up their telephones and call clients. Is it time to jump for joy? Are we going back to celebrating a bullish environment where investors are expected to receive 10% or greater returns? I think not, and I hope the following example proves why.

Imagine a situation where you have just moved to a new city and want to purchase a dry cleaning business. You find a dry cleaner for sale with a good reputation, modern equipment, honest and hardworking employees, and a long-term lease on the property. To keep this example simple, assume the business earns $100,000 per year. How much should you pay to buy the business at a fair price? Without taking into account other variables, such as "what-if" a new competitor moves into the neighborhood, you would probably pay a multiple of either the business earnings or its free cash flow. Net earnings is an accounting term that reflects what the business makes after paying taxes and interest costs, and deducting items such as depreciation, depletion, and amortization. Free cash flow is what the business has left over after spending money on all the expenditures and capital investments necessary to maintain the business.

For most businesses, the answer to the question of how much you should pay to acquire that business is a function of its expected future growth of cash flow and earnings. One way to determine the value of a business (without taking into consideration its assets) is to simply discount the future expected earnings and arrive at a current price. The math is easy, but getting the assumptions right about future economic growth, industry growth rates, competition, inflation, and expenses is often difficult. This is why Wall Street analysts are often unable to forecast earnings with a high degree of accuracy. If we were to estimate the future earnings and cash flow growth of our dry cleaner, what assumptions should we use?

The old mathematical models used to value assets still work, but the assumptions behind the numbers we put into those models must change to reflect a new economic order characterized by higher unemployment, massive underemployment, greater savings, and less spending. As of January 2011, the domestic economy is unlikely to grow rapidly anytime soon. The Federal Reserve is still keeping interest rates artificially low with the short-term Treasuries priced close to zero percent interest. This is akin to keeping a patient on life support. In this case, the patient is the U.S. economy, which is improving (for now) and technically coming out of a recession. But if you take away the life support now, the patient will die. Yes, the patient is improving but that improvement is relative.

Perhaps the smartest and best known fixed income manager in the world is PIMCO's Bill Gross. Gross, in an October 2009 letter to PIMCO investors, argued that asset prices at the current levels are 50% overvalued. He sees the global bond market yielding only 3.5%, with the current spreads (difference in yields between Treasuries and riskier bonds) reflecting the past and not current economic environment. Equities, in his opinion, will follow a 4% growth rate. He believes, as do I, that people investing under the assumption that valuations will return to the "old normal" are severely mistaken. Unfortunately, our little dry cleaner will not experience quick growth since it will not have the benefit of sharing in the quick growth of a rapidly improving U.S. economy anytime soon.

The dry cleaner is my anecdotal representation of our equity markets. As of October 2010, publicly traded domestic stocks were selling at an 18 times multiple to their earnings. In my example, the dry cleaner makes $100,000 per year in profits. If the dry cleaner were valued the way investors value publicly traded stocks, you would have to pay $1,800,000 for the business (18 x $100,000). That is a lot of money for a small business earning $100,000 per year! OK, I do understand that publicly traded companies should trade at a premium to privately held business concerns. After all, most publicly traded companies are liquid, meaning they can be bought and sold easily, unlike private companies that could take years to find the right buyer. Public companies also have better disclosure, at least in theory. But 18 times earnings? There must be a lot of future earnings and/or cash flow growth to justify paying that kind of multiple for our dry cleaner or any other company!

Unless our economy grows rapidly, stocks may be overvalued again! Yet many of the asset allocation models used by financial advisors still assume 10% returns on equities and the same economic growth that we saw during the past two decades. If I am right, investors using these models will continue to be disappointed.

So what should you pay for that dry cleaner? The answer is intuitive. Pay as little as possible to get your required return on the investment, and enough so the buyer will take your offer. The seller will gladly accept 18 times earnings, but you will never receive a good return on your money by paying $1,800,000 for $100,000 of income. Therefore, I would wait for the seller to lower the price. If he or she does not, then look for another business to purchase. And what should you pay if that dry cleaner were a publicly traded stock? The answer is the same. Pay as little as you can to get your required return on investment. You should willingly "pay up" for publicly traded stocks for the reason stated above, but not six or seven times more than private concerns. And that is why many common stocks are once again overpriced.

What happens to the business valuation if dividends are included in the dry cleaner scenario? Assume the dry cleaner pays its operator $100,000 in salary, and also pays its original investors $6,000 per year in dividends. Now what price should the business sell for? The inclusion of dividends will certainly increase the valuation of our small business, but by how much? That depends upon the reliability of the dividend stream, how fast the dividends are expected to grow, and the expected future yield of alternative investments.

Assume the dry cleaner's dividends are reliable but will not grow quickly because of the low expected growth rate of the local economy. Mathematics can then be easily used to find a fair market value. What mathematics cannot determine is investor preference. Some investors will gladly pay higher than the mathematically determined value if they cannot find stable 6% returns elsewhere. For example, if these investors think interest rates will start rising for a long period of time due to inflation, their natural inclination will be to avoid fixed income securities (bonds) that lose money when interest rates rise, and instead purchase dividend producing businesses.

This example shows why dividend producing stocks make sense in a market characterized by high forward price/earnings multiples. Even if valuations change temporarily for the worse, investors can take comfort in a steady dividend stream that provides income and helps the price stability of the stock.

Years ago, a dairy farmer in the Catskills told me a story that taught me about the importance of a dividend stream. He said, "In the old days you bought a cow when you needed milk. The price of the cow would always change a little bit over time, but nobody cared very much as long as the cow was still producing milk." I believe investors in dry cleaners and stocks can learn from this story, and that is no bull.

CHAPTER 6

FIXED INCOME AFTER 2008
The End of 30 Good Years for Bonds

A wealthy medical professional I know sold out of stocks several months before the equity markets began to crash in 2008. He now wishes to remain "conservative" with his investments and asked my opinion about keeping the majority of his assets in government and high quality corporate bonds. He was quite surprised when I told him that high quality fixed income investments are now one of the most dangerous places to invest, and will likely remain a risky place to invest for some time.

In the words of PIMCO's Bill Gross, who many consider the most knowledgeable and finest fixed income manager alive, we are investing in an economic environment that is the "New Normal." In the "New Normal" our expected economic growth and expected returns from investments are lower than what we experienced over most of the past forty years. Many of the rules that governed our investment decisions in the past no longer apply. Gross also believes the United States economy is in a fearsome bind that economists call a "liquidity trap."

Why are we in a New Normal? The massive deleveraging since the fall of 2008 is one reason. Investment returns we enjoyed on our real estate and financial assets turned out to be in part from financial leverage, and that leverage is now disappearing.

Deleveraging leads initially to a lower level of economic activity since business and consumer lending decline. Less economic activity leads to fewer tax receipts. For the first time in nearly 60 years, U.S. receipts (revenue from taxes) are less than what the government is spending for our benefit, further increasing our country's deficits. Most economists believe our already massive deficits, along with the recent historic bailouts orchestrated by our Federal Reserve, will someday be inflationary.

Another important factor is the "liquidity trap." In a classic liquidity trap interest rates can no longer be dropped to further stimulate the economy since they are already at the lowest possible levels. In this situation, the only alternatives are to let the economy deflate (the Federal Reserve and our politicians deem this impractical) or print money. The printing of money, also called "writing checks" or "monetary easing," is inflationary. Should this inflation occur, and it seems as though it will, our interest rates will naturally rise. Rising interest rates are very bad for the prices of fixed income.

Investing in fixed income securities (bonds) can be complicated. There are many types of fixed income investments to choose from as well as a variety of ways to take a position in the asset class. Some examples of fixed income securities are individual bonds, mutual funds, exchange traded funds, and unit investment trusts. As with all investments, investing in fixed income comes with various risks that should be familiar to investors: default risk (the risk of the issuer defaulting on the bond and not paying the principal or interest); call risk (the risk of the issuer legally calling in the bond and paying back principal before the term of the bond); and interest rate risk (the risk of a rise in interest rates causing a temporary reduction in the value of existing fixed income securities held by investors).

Why do rising interest rates hurt bondholders? A 10-year Treasury bond today can be purchased at a yield of approximately 2.60%. Treasury securities are considered safe investments (no credit or default risk) since they are backed by the full faith and credit of the U.S. government. If you purchase that bond you can rest assured the government will make timely interest and principal payments to you. Unlike any state government, bank or other corporation, the U.S. government can always print more money if it needs it. But what if interest rates rise to 4.60% (still a low interest rate in post-WWII historic terms) in a few years because the government's continued desire to print money becomes inflationary? That simple 2.00% rise in interest rates from the 2.60% base equates to a 77% increase in interest rates! Using a complicated formula involving the concept of "duration," those bonds could easily decline in value by 20% or more, depending upon how many years were left to maturity.

The good news is that the decrease in value would be temporary if you own individual bonds—the value will creep back to par value as the bond approaches maturity. Of course, owning a 30-year bond would be more problematic than a 10-year bond because it could take 30 years to sell that bond at par if interest rates started rising soon after you bought it. Most investors I know do not want to wait 30 years to break even on any of their investments!

The assurance that a fixed income investment will eventually go back to par is not necessarily true if you own bonds in a mutual fund. Mutual funds commingle your assets with those from other people, and hire a portfolio manager to oversee the investments. As interest rates rise, most fixed income mutual funds lose money, and this can create problems for the fund managers and shareholders. Some shareholders, unhappy with losing money, will naturally want to sell their shares in the bond funds. When this happens, the fund managers will have to sell bonds to match the daily liquidations. There is no chance to hold onto a bond and wait for it to go to par once a fund manager sells it for a loss to meet daily liquidations! Therefore, the remaining investors in those mutual funds will probably end up with principal losses that will never be recovered in their lifetimes.

Why do investment advisors continue to place their clients' money in bond funds, 529 plans (that invest in bond funds), fixed income sub-accounts within variable annuities, and asset allocation programs that utilize bond funds? The answer has to do with tradition, the business model of investment advisors, and the improper reliance on asset classes (like bonds) reverting to their average returns over a reasonable time period.

Asset allocation based on Modern Portfolio Theory does not work in the "New Normal" because assets no longer have the same long-term "mean" value to return to in an economic environment characterized by deleveraging. One example of why asset allocation no longer works is fixed income. The 30-year bull market in fixed income has ended, and the beginning of a long-term bear market in bonds is just beginning. Therefore, taking the past 30-year performance of bonds as a basis for investing in them in an asset allocation model is foolish and a recipe for investment failure!

What are the best ways for you to obtain a safe and reliable income stream in the post-2008 investment environment?

1. Equities, for the first time since the 1940's, are yielding more than bonds. Some of these stocks, exchange traded funds, and publicly traded partnerships are now being considered by many investors as fixed income substitutes. Does this mean stocks are now as safe as bonds? No! But investor preferences to avoid fixed income investments may well mean there is now a valuation floor beneath many higher quality dividend producing equities.

2. Annuities are usually higher yielding than government bonds and are backed by the issuing insurance company. Annuities are complex for many reasons, yet they are a reasonable alternative for those looking for fixed income alternatives.

3. Treasury bonds that are indexed to inflation have become the preferred investment for many fixed income investors. Treasury Inflation-Protected bonds (TIPS) are indexed to inflation (and deflation should it occur) as judged by the Consumer Price Index. Since inflation is the main reason why domestic interest rates will rise, TIPS are considered a hedge against rising interest rates.

4. Lower duration fixed income investments, if held to maturity, should also be considered for inclusion in investor portfolios. These investments can be used within several different fixed income portfolio strategies.

5. Non-U.S. dollar denominated bonds, tied to currencies of countries expected to inflate less than the United States, offer protection. Investing prudently in emerging market debt can help boost the yield of fixed income portfolios.

6. Purchasing lower duration corporate and agency securities, with higher yields than Treasuries, also will help boost yield.

The New Normal portends a low return environment, a low economic growth rate, and the continuation of our massive deficits (and the corresponding printing of money by the Federal Reserve). This environment will be inflationary. As investors in the 1970's remember, inflation destroys the value of long-term bonds. Now is the time to reposition your portfolios in advance of the coming inflation.

CHAPTER 7

DISINTERMEDIATION
What Asset Management Really Costs You

Many investors have lost or not made money over the past decade, yet they pay ongoing fees to their financial advisors and the investment managers their advisors recommend. Investment managers of mutual funds, separate accounts, and insurance company sub-accounts charge fees in addition to trading, legal, accounting, auditing, and reporting costs. In addition to those fees and costs, investors commonly pay 1% or greater in fees to their financial advisors for overseeing the investment strategy. For most clients, the cornerstone of their investment strategy was and is asset allocation – a fundamentally flawed approach that failed to protect investors in the debacle of 2008.

For example, if your financial advisor charges a 1% advisory fee combined with mutual funds or separate account management fees averaging another 1%, then you are paying 2% or more per year in total fees. The impact of these fees on the value of your portfolio is significant, particularly in a low return environment. Using simple arithmetic, these fees cost your account about 20% of its market value over a 10-year period. This is very costly in time periods when your account does not make money! Even if your investment advisor uses index funds with management fees of 0.25%, the 10-year loss in account value is still significant when including the 1% advisory fee. Is there a less expensive way to invest in the long run? I believe there is, as long as advisors charge lower fees commensurate with the service they provide, and low cost financial intermediaries (investment managers) are used.

Convincing your financial advisor to charge lower fees may be difficult because the 1% advisory fee is still the industry standard. Also, it is highly unlikely for a larger wirehouse or bank to lower its published fee schedule. But it is possible for the firm to grant exceptions, especially if faced with losing your account to a competitor. Independent planners are more likely to negotiate fees with you depending upon services provided. If your advisor provides financial planning and investment advice, then the 1% investment advisory fee might be considered reasonable, even if the total return outlook for stocks is less than 10% per year.

In addition to advisory fees, there are the costs from "intermediation." Where on earth did the terms "intermediation" and "disintermediation" come from? In the late 1970's, individual investors found they could get higher interest rates by purchasing Treasury bills, notes and bonds directly from the U. S. government instead of from a financial intermediary (a bank or broker) in the secondary market. Investors also avoided the commissions or transaction fees associated with the purchase of Treasury securities through banks or brokers. The elimination of costly financial intermediaries became known as "disintermediation."

By the mid-1980's, Wall Street figured out how to make billions of dollars in annual profits through a type of intermediation that was different from what the banks provided. During this time investors saw a bull market in both stocks and bonds, which made many quickly forget the disastrous 1968-1982 investment period. Mutual funds became the most popular investment of the time, and they still are. Assets in mutual funds rose from less than $150 billion in 1982 to over $10 trillion in 2007! After 2000, many advisors had a new product to sell: separate account management. Separate account management became popular with the general public when investment managers reduced the typical minimums from $1 million (or more) to as low as $100,000, making these types of accounts more accessible to the average investor. Insurance companies also got into the game with variable life insurance and variable annuity products.

"Asset allocation" was the excuse Wall Street needed to provide lots of financial intermediation (read: profits). For a fee—usually 1% on top of the fees charged by investment managers—financial advisors offered to:

1. Write an investment policy statement for each client.

2. Choose investment managers who they hoped would "beat the relevant index" and "provide safety during bear markets."

3. Monitor portfolios for performance and regularly "rebalance" the account in line with a predetermined asset mix.

But did investors get anything for their 1%? I think not! This is why I believe disintermediation will become a hot topic again in the wake of the market crash of 2008.

Many clients did not receive an optimal investment strategy because the governing "investment policy statement" was not a true investment policy. It was merely a computerized conduit into the asset allocation platform sold by the advisor and/or the advisor's firm. Clients, unfortunately, were not informed that their "custom" investment policy statement consisted of only one investment strategy: asset allocation. Also, many clients were not aware that their investment strategy depended solely upon past history and not prevailing social, economic, and political expectations.

It is unreasonable to pay an advisor 1% of the market value of your assets, and expect him or her to choose investment managers who will consistently outperform the market. Statistically, it is almost impossible to find investment managers who can beat the market without analyzing twenty or more years of historical performance data from each manager!

Even if a financial advisor finds a manager who can beat the relevant index, the advisor still has to analyze how and why the manager did so—did the manager take more risk or have good security selection skills? Also, the advisor must feel confident that the manager can outperform the benchmark after fees in the future. Finally, he has to understand the manager's investment style and be comfortable that it will "fit" into the relevant style box of the advisor's asset allocation model.

This is virtually an impossible task, given that study after study shows that at least 80% of active managers (mutual fund, separate account, etc.) do not beat their relevant index in any given year. Therefore, investors can beat 80% of the active managers 100% of the time by using index funds (passively managed accounts), and paying substantially less than the usual 2% (or more) for management and advisory fees.

Contrary to the last paragraph, I do believe there are a handful of equity and fixed income managers who can and do beat the markets on a regular basis. However, I also believe these managers are successful because they purposely do not lock themselves into an asset allocation "style box" that would force them to match the volatility and universe of securities to the "style." For example, I once asked Charles Brandes, the founder of a highly successful investment management firm, if he attempts to track the volatility of any particular value index or fit within a "style box." His answer was simple enough: "We find opportunities, buy them at a substantial discount to their intrinsic value, and that's it." Brandes's separate accounts are popular with financial advisors because his pure value approach has historically performed well. I find it interesting that financial advisors who pretend to be "asset allocators" use his accounts in light of his firm having no desire to match the volatility and co-variance of a particular "style" box or index.

Investors can easily and prudently lower the costs associated with their investments. The cost of investing in *any financial product* has never been as inexpensive as it is today, providing you choose the lowest cost option. Passive investors can invest in index funds with total annual fees of 0.40% or less to avoid the cost of active management. Passive investors going it alone (without financial advisors) can avoid fees charged to "asset allocate" by investing in equities through global or total market indexes, and then adding fixed income through low-cost closed-end funds, exchange traded funds or direct investments. Investors with active strategies can lower costs by avoiding expensive mutual funds and investing in exchange traded funds, no-load funds, separate account managers, certain closed-end funds, and individual securities.

Wall Street has made a fortune on your money for years (that is what it does). Some of the financial products, services, and investment strategies offered by Wall Street are fairly priced and some are overpriced. When the financial net worth of the investor improves, the money earned by Wall Street through those financial products and investment strategies is reasonable and justified. When the fees charged are not commensurate with the value or return received by the investor, those services are not fairly priced. Based upon the returns investors received over the past ten years, investors are paying too much to have their money managed.

Investors looking for greater returns should only pay-up for investment products and strategies that are customized and work better than passively investing in an index. In the future, prudent financial advisors will assist investors by finding lower-cost investments and by investing directly in securities (disintermediation).

CHAPTER 8

THE *WHO* BEHIND YOU

Everyone has their own views about money. Some people feel uncomfortable thinking or talking about money. Other people feel money is important to maintain financial independence or to provide a margin of safety for their loved ones. Power is the reason some love money. To others, money is all about self-importance. I believe the idea of using the same computerized investment strategy for all investors is absolutely ridiculous given we all think about money differently. In fact, the way we think about money should be the basis for determining a prudent investment strategy. But how do we characterize how we think about money in a way that is useful for investing?

There are many ways to characterize how we think. Every day we are bombarded with ideas for how to think about our money and manage our assets. Popular books, television and radio news programs, talk shows, and even infomercials provide us with some insight on these topics. I have found two ideas that are superior for helping you think about your money:

1. Write your own obituary.

2. Define your psychological approach to money.

The first may seem controversial and somewhat disturbing, but it is brutally effective. Writing your own obituary (no one else has to see it) forces you to determine how others will eventually view your life. Many people tend to procrastinate when it comes time to making important personal and financial decisions. Sometimes we wait so long that we miss important opportunities. Decisions are made by default rather than in accordance with your desires or wishes. This exercise serves as a catalyst for the process by helping you determine what is truly important to you, and what memories or legacy you wish to leave for others. It is easier to make meaningful personal and financial decisions once you determine what is really important to you now and in the future.

I did this exercise several years ago. Writing my obituary helped me decide that I want to spend more time with my family instead of constantly traveling for a large corporation. It also helped me clarify my charitable giving goals, and my desire to have an enjoyable and profitable practice rather than a hard-to-manage business. If you are having trouble making decisions in your life, financial or otherwise, taking time to write your obit may prove helpful.

The second idea comes from Russ Alan Prince and Karen Maru File, and it is based on their research of high net worth psychology, which was funded by *Institutional Investor Magazine* over a decade ago. Their statistically significant research showed how people view their personal wealth and the reasons why they gift their money. Prince taught me about the psychology of money when he was a consultant for a large financial institution where I once worked. For the purposes of this book, I will focus only on the psychology of personal wealth.

Prince and File probed the psychological reasons why people invest and identified nine investor psychologies or personalities:

1. Family Stewards

2. Financial Phobics

3. Financial Independents

4. Anonymous

5. Moguls

6. V.I.P.s

7. Accumulators

8. Gamblers

9. Innovators

I have found that some individuals fit perfectly into one of these categories, while others are a composite of several personalities. The following section provides a brief summary of each category.

Family Stewards

The "Family Steward" is most interested in creating and using wealth to take care of his or her spouse, children, future generations and charities. Family Stewards tend to avoid conspicuous displays of wealth and are not likely to buy and drive the fanciest cars. Showing off their money in their day-to-day clothing or jewelry is not of great importance to them.

Family Stewards want to know everything will be taken care of in the event of their disability or demise. Investment strategies that will do this are paramount, as are investment strategies that require minimum modification over time. Guaranteed investment strategies and asset-liability matching are of great interest to Family Stewards, as are "set it and forget it" investment strategies like asset allocation. Unfortunately, asset allocation did not perform as well as Family Stewards had hoped or anticipated.

Financial Phobics

"Financial Phobics" have fears about money. They enjoy making money but simply do not like thinking about it. Typical Financial Phobics are afraid to look at their brokerage statements and do not have the necessary Wills and Trusts that would be beneficial to their heirs and charities. If married, chances are their spouses are not financially phobic and find their lack of financial interest frustrating.

Financial Phobics have special needs from a financial planning and investment perspective. First and foremost, they need to be protected against fraud and expensive, mediocre strategies because they are not comfortable reviewing their accounts on a regular basis. They must have written strategies that are easy to understand and execute, with greater diversification than would typically be considered "prudent." They should consider having a spouse or another family member help them monitor their investments since they are unlikely to do this themselves.

Financial Independents

The main goal of "Financial Independents" is to avoid relying on or depending on others for financial or any other kind of support. This group of high net worth individuals does not wish to go to their children or others for assistance in their later years. As a result, Financial Independents with a multi-million dollar liquid net worth will pre-pay for everything (e.g., burial plots, long-term care and health insurance, retirement homes, assisted living facilities, newspaper subscriptions) so that their children will never be bothered.

Ensuring their goal of independence is paramount in their minds. Financial Independents enjoy guaranteed investments, insurance, and dependable investment strategies characterized by a high probability of success.

Anonymous

Some people prefer to maintain a low profile or be "Anonymous" when it comes to money matters. There are many different reasons why they feel the need to be secretive or private about their finances. A lottery winner may not want to display his wealth for fear that his friends will treat him differently. A wealthy inheritor may feel that she does not deserve the money and prefers to give it away quietly. A wealthy business owner may require financial secrecy because he is concerned with his family's safety or does not want to be bothered by people asking him for donations or loans. Regardless of the reasons, the Anonymous require confidentiality in their financial affairs. The Anonymous prefer financial strategies that can be quietly executed without drawing attention to themselves. They tend to invest through trusts or partnerships (without their names on them) and have few trusted advisors.

Moguls

"Moguls" like to be in control. I have a "Mogul" friend who could have retired years ago, yet he continues to work for one reason: power (or perceived power, as the case may be). He enjoys making decisions and developing strategies. His money gives him the freedom to do this inside his business, with his family, and with the charities he is involved with. As you might guess, he and other Moguls drive powerful black cars, are intolerant of mediocrity, and have little time for small talk.

Moguls prefer investment strategies they can control. They

require a summary of information to make the final decision on all aspects of their financial affairs. For example, a Mogul who wants a large insurance policy for business purposes will ask his assistant, advisor or agent to review all the available products, summarize the best priced insurance policies, and provide the financial rating for each company. He will also request a complete, detailed analysis of how to finance or pay for the insurance, and will look at the summary before he tells the agent which product to use.

V.I.P.s

"V.I.P.s" need money to feel special and enjoy life. Only the best that money can buy will do for V.I.P.s. They cannot be happy without money and the luxurious trappings that go along with having money. Money gives them access to "important" people, great events where they can be "seen," and the best of everything that is necessary to them. I find that V.I.P.s are usually very special in several ways other than their money, but they do not necessarily realize it.

There are examples of V.I.P.s everywhere. *The Real Housewives* television series is about the lives of wealthy V.I.P. women in major cities. Love him or hate him, wealth makes Donald Trump feel special and allows him to market his luxury real estate and other businesses. Paris Hilton, whose Internet porn tape and stint in jail made her the poster child for those who oppose the elimination of the estate tax, would not feel good living her party lifestyle without money.

V.I.P.s want the best, and only the best-known money managers will satisfy them. Advisors need to protect V.I.P.s by using diligence and care when analyzing investments and investment managers. For example, investing with a hedge fund manager who was a big name on Wall Street made sense for many V.I.P.s until the Madoff name became synonymous with fraud!

Accumulators

"Accumulators" like keeping score, and they do it through their net worth. Unlike V.I.P.s, Accumulators do not need to show off with lots of fancy toys. They simply want a bigger number on the bottom of the asset side of their balance sheet every year.

A portfolio manager once told me a story about a well-known hedge fund manager who slept on his office sofa at night waiting for the markets to open. Even though he was worth several hundred million dollars, the fact that a former classmate was a billionaire drove him crazy. He had to make more money! Most Accumulators are not that extreme, but they do want to see positive results on a consistent basis. Warren Buffett is perhaps the best known Accumulator. He purposely decided not to give away his wealth (to the Gates Foundation) until he was older. As a "high compounding" investor, Buffett correctly assumed he would have more money to give away by waiting.

Accumulators require investment strategies that offer an extreme likelihood of positive annual returns. I find that younger Accumulators are willing to take substantial risk (though they do not perceive it as such) to increase their net worth, while older ones prefer to take less risk and are generally happier to settle for lower returns.

Innovators

"Innovators" live to create and change things for the better. Their wealth is not about power, independence, ego, confidentiality, or their balance sheet. More wealth allows these investors to innovate even more, giving their lives more purpose. The fields of technology and the arts are filled with Innovators. In Silicon Valley, some Innovators are changing the traditional ways of charitable giving.

Innovators do not view their wealth as the end-all and be-all of their lives. They envision wealth as a tool for their next project (business or charitable). Many Innovators are not interested in long-term strategies since their money may be needed for another idea once it presents itself. They need new and exciting "cutting edge" investment strategies to be happy. Asset allocation is not interesting enough for most Innovators, but certain hedge fund strategies may be attractive to them.

Gamblers

"Gamblers" represent roughly 5% of the investment population. They love money because it allows them to keep taking risks, which gives them the requisite shot of euphoria they need to stay happy.

All of us know of Gamblers who made fortunes, lost them, and made them back again. For example, legendary oilman T. Boone Pickens is a Gambler who at one point was a billionaire, lost most of his money, and then became a billionaire again.

Gamblers love commodities, options, and anything else associated with leverage. Good ones have a knack of knowing when the odds are in their favor and then enjoy "throwing all their chips into the pot." Poor ones always find a way to lose their money. Gamblers, and their seemingly reckless investment strategies, are a financial advisor's nightmare. Those strategies often expose the Gambler and their advisors to increased regulatory scrutiny and potential lawsuits.

Many high net worth investors fit into one category, while other investors are best described as a combination of several categories. It is certainly possible for personalities to change over time, particularly after a significant event.

Couples with different psychological personality types are very interesting to me. Oftentimes, they cannot find a middle ground regarding their money until they understand the differences in their high net worth personalities. Then they can find a way to save and invest that is suitable to both parties.

I firmly believe that determining the "who behind you" is the critical first step toward creating your investment strategy. There are many ways to develop an investment strategy but knowing the "who behind you" will help you identify the optimal strategy that "feels" right and allows you to sleep at night.

CHAPTER 9

AVOIDING DUBIOUS SCHEMES AND FRAUD

The act of investing in domestic and international securities with different market capitalizations and investment styles (growth, value, foreign, etc.) *did not provide* suitable diversification during the market crash of 2008. Simply put, when the economy began to collapse, most asset classes became "correlated" and lost value in concert with each other. "Asset allocation" was the typical diversification technique of the day, and asset allocation absolutely did not protect investors. I believe the "asset allocation" method of diversification will fail to protect investors in the future. Finding a better way to diversify your portfolio is more important and more challenging than ever before.

We are in a low return environment for stocks, real estate, and fixed income. These investments are unlikely to generate the double-digit returns many investors seek. The good news is there are many alternative ways to invest money, diversify your portfolio, and provide a suitable income stream. The returns from alternative investments may not be higher than more traditional investments, but at least diversification is added.

The bad news is a low return environment gives criminals and con artists ample opportunity to create and perpetuate investment scams by convincingly suggesting "safe and guaranteed" high return strategies just for you! These "confidence games" have been around for centuries, and as long as people are greedy, these scams will never disappear. Before we explore my technique for identifying scams, a review of some of the more famous "Ponzi" schemes is in order.

Nearly eighty years before Bernard Madoff became a household name, a man with a criminal past put together a scam that made him the most infamous swindler in American history. Carlo Pietro Giovanni Guglielmo Tebaldo Ponzi, an Italian immigrant better known as Charles Ponzi, was certainly not the first person to rip off the public using a "rob Peter to pay Paul" scheme. Yet his brazen use of this scheme permanently etched his name in history and made his name synonymous with this type of scam.

Ponzi served time in two jails for forgery and for illegal smuggling of immigrants before moving to Boston in 1911. After WWI, he thought he found a way to arbitrage Internal Reply Coupons (IRC), which were given by letter writers to their recipients for return postage. Many world governments honored IRCs after WWI. Since postage rates varied greatly between countries, he saw a great opportunity to purchase IRCs in Italy and sell them to U.S. citizens for a large percentage profit. His idea would have modestly worked if the "red tape" (handling fees) were not so high. Regardless, Ponzi convinced his marks that investing in his IRC scheme would produce 400% profits and double their invested money every 90 days. He used the money from new investors to pay the original investors interest, and word quickly spread about his "financial acumen." Money poured into his Securities Exchange Company, making Charles Ponzi a million-aire within a few months. Soon he became the largest depositor in the Hanover Trust Bank of Boston.

Of course the plan was destined to fail. A local newspaper, the *Post,* hired the well-known financial writer Clarence Barron (founder of *Barron's*) to investigate the scheme. Barron correctly calculated that Ponzi would have to be investing in over 150 million IRCs with the money he raised even though less than

30 thousand IRCs were in circulation. Eventually, the state bank commissioner and attorney general became involved and the scheme, now known as a "Ponzi scheme," collapsed.

None of this stopped Charles Ponzi. After spending time in jail, Ponzi relocated to Jacksonville, Florida, where he was arrested for selling swampland while promising investors 200% returns within a few months time. After serving his time in a Florida prison, he moved back to Italy and was hired by Mussolini to work for, believe it or not, the Italian Treasury. He promptly left the country after stealing money from the Treasury and died a penniless man in South America. One would think the schemes named after Charles Ponzi would have ended by now. Unfortunately, Ponzi schemes rob investors every day!

Ponzi was not the only famous man involved in scams. Scam artists come from every country, represent both sexes, and are members of every religious group. Examples include Pakistani Syed Sibtul Hassan Shaho, whose stock investment program bilked investors out of nearly $900 million. Maria Branca dos Santos ("Dona" Branca) was known as "The People's Banker" and operated a banking scheme in Portugal for nearly 15 years before she entered prison. Her bank was built on the deposits of the common person, whom she promised to help. Russia's largest scam artist to date is Sergey Mavrodi, who actually became a member of its parliament. Mavrodi and his brother bilked over two million investors for more than $1.5 billion. Mavrodi promised dividends of up to 100%. In the beginning, he delivered on that promise by using $11 million per day in new investments to pay off earlier investors. Mavrodi was eventually caught and sent to a penal colony.

China is now the hotbed for pyramid and Ponzi schemes, despite the potential threat of the death penalty for economic crimes and fraud. A man named Wang Fengyou was recently arrested for bilking over $1 billion from investors who spent money to buy ant farms. Wang promised investors large returns by first purchasing and then cultivating his specialty ants. When the ants died, he agreed to buy them back, giving the investors huge profits. The dead ants, he claimed, would be used for various types of herbal medicine, including aphrodisiacs. Similar to Charles Ponzi, Wang used money from new investors to pay "profits" to the earlier investors before the scheme began to unravel. A year before a fellow countryman named Wang Zhendong was sentenced to death for propagating a similar ant farming scam and bilking investors for more than $400 million. Financial fraud is no small matter in China.

All these Ponzi schemes were large in their scope, but none equaled the duration and size ($65 billion) of the one pulled off by Bernard "Bernie" Madoff. Bernie Madoff ran a firm that bore his name and put a new twist on the Ponzi scheme by offering investors modest returns through a relatively "safe" arbitrage scheme (arbitrage is certainly legal). His firm, like many hedge funds, required a large minimum investment that excluded the general public. Over 4,800 investors and institutions anted-up the $20 million minimum investment necessary to invest with Bernie.

What was so shocking about the fall of Bernie Madoff was the trust Wall Street had in him, along with the size and duration of the fraud. It was easy to trust a man who headed a longstanding Wall Street institution—he founded Bernard Madoff Investment Securities in 1960. It was easy to trust a man whose firm was once the largest market maker in the United States. It was easy to trust a man who was well known to all the major market participants and was even the chairman of the NASDAQ. It was easy to trust a major philanthropist who believed in good causes. It was easy for investors to trust Madoff with an estimated $65 billion of their money, although the actual size of the fraud may be less because much of the $65 billion figure consisted of phony gains.

Most investors thought his "split-strike conversion strategy" was difficult but not impossible to execute. They were not alarmed when he did not provide details about his strategy—"black box" investors rarely disclose their mathematical algorithms. However, there was at least one financial analyst, Harry Markopolos, who was alarmed by Madoff's reported numbers.

In late 1999 and early 2000, Markopolos was asked by his Boston employer, Rampart Investment Management Company, Inc., to review the viability of Madoff's strategy and determine whether it could be duplicated. Markopolos was the perfect man for the task. He is a Chartered Financial Analyst and a Certified Fraud Examiner with a background in forensic accounting (forensic accountants are adept at finding fraudulent activities). Similar to Clarence Barron's analysis of Ponzi's operation, Markopolos determined the option market was not big enough for Madoff to execute his "split-strike conversion strategy," and Markopolos concluded something was amiss. Markopolos guessed Madoff was front-running (placing trades in front of clients) and/or engaging in a Ponzi scheme. Since front running alone could not explain the reported profits, he was convinced Madoff was running a Ponzi operation.

Harry Markopolos anonymously contacted the U.S. Securities and Exchange Commission (SEC) in late 1999 about the fraud. They showed no interest in his findings. He later contacted them in person and was still not believed. He thought about contacting the Financial Industry Regulatory Association (FINRA) but decided not to because Bernie Madoff's brother, Peter, was FINRA's Vice Chairman. In late 2005, Markopolos sent a 21 page memo detailing his findings to Meaghan Cheung, a branch chief at the SEC. Surprisingly, the SEC still showed no interest in his findings! Cheung resigned shortly thereafter.

The rest is history. Bernie Madoff is now known as running the largest and longest Ponzi scheme on the planet and will likely spend the rest of his days behind bars. The SEC has a new head, who boasts an impressive resume. Mary L. Schapiro has asked

Congress for more money to provide better enforcement. Congress is debating how to provide better regulatory oversight of Wall Street, with the blessing of the Obama administration.

So what happened to all the money? That is still to be determined. I doubt much of it is still in the United States or in Swiss bank accounts, because the Swiss government is now more open to working with U.S. regulatory agencies. My guess is Madoff copied the way organized crime launders money by setting up a string of fictitious entities overseas and transferring funds to those entities. This may explain why he pleaded guilty to all charges. He refused to cooperate with authorities and has no obligation to help them locate the stolen money.

I believe Ponzi schemes are still around us today, perhaps growing in number because of the weakened economy. Investors have to be more vigilant than ever to avoid them.

The following headlines are from some of the 2009 SEC press releases on the SEC website:

SEC Charges Georgia Attorney for Conducting Multi-Million Dollar Ponzi Scheme

Colorado Advisor Charged by SEC for Conducting Multi-Million Dollar Ponzi Scheme

SEC Obtains Asset Freeze in Ponzi Scheme Targeting Chinese-American Community in Dallas Area

It seems the SEC is embarrassed about the Madoff affair and is openly publicizing any success against fraud!

I recently cautioned a lawyer friend about investing in a scheme advertised on a local radio station that suggested investors will earn a "12%-14% return guaranteed by some of the safest companies in the world." The scheme could be legitimate, but I have serious concerns about the promised returns. The promoter does not have audited financials available to the public (I called and asked for them). There is a lack of liquidity in this particular type of investment. The promoter's reported returns are greater than the historical returns of the industry. The promoter does not consider the investment a "security" under The Securities Act of 1933. Most importantly, the promoter's need to involve the public (and not institutions) as investors frightens me. Institutions regularly invest $250 million or more in this type of investment program. Why, then, does the promoter need individual investors' money?

I sent an e-mail to the radio station that advertised the investment and offered reasons why I believe the returns suggested by the promoter are unlikely to be realized by the investors. The radio station had no interest and is still broadcasting the same advertisement despite the logical information I outlined in the e-mail. Now I know how Harry Markopolos must have felt!

How do you avoid disappointing investments, Ponzi schemes, and other financial frauds? Here is some general advice:

1. Remember that anything that sounds too good to be true probably is. Most Ponzi schemes come from people offering above market returns and requiring their victims to do nothing more than writing a check. We should all know by now that there is rarely a free lunch!

2. Always know the third-party custodian of your funds; and then verify your funds are there. For example, let us assume your financial advisor custodies his client accounts at Charles Schwab (nothing wrong with that). You should make certain your checks for investments are endorsed to "Charles Schwab" and your statements come from Charles Schwab. To be safe, call the custodian to ensure the assets are there, making certain that no one made up a statement that was mailed to you.

3. Read your financial statements every month. About the only way an advisor can steal money from you when your

funds are with a third-party custodian is by forging your signature on checks or wire transfers.

4. Think twice before granting full power of attorney for check-writing or bill-paying to anyone. If you do, make certain a system of checks and balances is in place. This is particularly important for elderly investors who use other advisors (accountants, financial advisors, attorneys, etc.) to pay their bills.

5. Ask lots of questions before investing in any illiquid alternative strategy. Know the background of the manager, understand the investment strategy, ask for bank and other references, know who audits the financial reports, etc.

6. Ask yourself, "Why does the promoter of an investment need me?" The answer will weed out the potential for most fraud. For example, a mutual fund or separate account manager makes his or her money by charging modest fees to many investors, and there is nothing wrong with that. They need your assets because charging a management fee to many investors is how they earn their money.

7. Ask yourself, "How easy is it for the promoter to institute a Ponzi scheme or other fraud?" For example, you may want to invest in hard assets (gold, platinum, etc.) for diversification or as a future inflation hedge. There are several ways to take a position in hard assets, including mutual funds (commodity producing stocks), exchange traded funds, and gold coins. There is little chance of fraud with investing in funds, but there is a good chance of fraud by purchasing coins. If you actually buy gold coins, who holds onto them (the custodian)? Who determines the appraised value when they are purchased? What is the spread between the bid and offer price? Is it possible new investors are needed to pay off existing ones? How easy is

it to sell your investment? In one case, an investor in gold coins found the spread between the bid and offer price for his coins was in excess of 30%. Worse, the promoter appraised his own inventory! The investor found out the hard way that it is often better to invest in ways that are liquid rather than illiquid. Liquidity is usually a good defense against fraud.

8. Ask for the promoter's audited financial statements. Consider walking away if you cannot get any statements.

9. Ask for the audited financial statements of the next "great opportunity" anyone wants you to invest in. Then look at the firm's cash flow from operations (CFFO) for the past few years. If CFFO is decreasing while sales and earnings are increasing, beware. Double beware.

Financial fraud is more prevalent than ever. If the federal, state, and industry regulators could not stop Bernie Madoff for decades, you cannot expect them to stop a Ponzi scheme promoted through your local house of worship, a radio advertisement, word of mouth, or a financial advisor who "forgot" that a large commission eliminated the need for due diligence. And do not forget the biggest "rob Peter to pay Paul" scheme of them all called Social Security. That scheme will last for a long, long time because Congress can always extend the age before full benefits are paid. At least with Social Security, retirees are guaranteed to get some of their money back, even if it is not what they paid into it.

CHAPTER 10

LIFE INSURANCE AFTER 2008

I entered the financial industry in the late 1970's, a time of high interest rates and high inflation. Almost all life insurance sold was either term or whole life.

Term insurance is temporary insurance. A stated premium is paid for a specified number of years of coverage after which the policy lapses. In some cases, the term policy can be continued or extended after the period expires, but the original rates and conditions are not guaranteed. The new premiums are usually higher, reflecting the cost of insurance at the time of the new period.

Whole life insurance is more expensive than term insurance because it is designed to provide coverage for the *whole* life of the insured. It is permanent insurance characterized by a level premium guaranteed to provide insurance coverage and to provide a cash value equal to the face amount at a stated age, usually 100. The face amount is the stated amount of insurance coverage that is paid to the beneficiaries upon the death of the insured. The level premiums for whole life insurance are higher than the cost of insurance during the early years of the contract, when the "excess" premium is used to build cash value. This cash value is used to pay part of the premium (sometimes all of it) in the later years of the contract when the cost of insurance rises substantially with the insured's age.

If properly structured, whole life offers some interesting advantages:

- The cash value in the policy grows tax deferred.

- The insurance proceeds (death benefits) are generally paid to the beneficiaries free of income tax.

- Potential estate taxes and probate costs may be avoided if the policy is owned by another person (someone other than the insured), a charity, or an irrevocable trust, and the transfer did not take place within three years of the insured's death.

- There are several beneficial options for the use of policy dividends.

- The policy owner may borrow against the cash value of the policy during the insured's lifetime.

In the late 1970's, holders of whole life insurance discovered an interesting arbitrage. They borrowed against the cash value of their insurance policies at the very low interest rates stated in their policies, and invested that money elsewhere. Policyholders were able to borrow at 3% from a guaranteed investment (their life insurance) and invest at 10% or more in another guaranteed investment (U.S. Treasuries). Insurance companies, however, cannot earn investment income on borrowed money. The insurance industry attempted to stop the arbitrage by marketing a new type of permanent policy, universal life insurance.

Universal life (UL) insurance combines the low cost protection of term insurance with a savings component. The cash value (the savings component) is invested tax deferred within the UL contract, and may be available for a loan to the policyholder. The key advantage of a UL policy is flexibility, allowing the policy owner to shift money between the savings and insurance portions of the policy. This flexibility is particularly beneficial in years of high interest rates, when the cash value grows faster. The policyholder may use the cash value to either increase the death benefit (premiums remain the same) or lower the premiums (no change in death benefit).

August of 1982 marked the beginning of the greatest bull market of the century. The 1980's were also a time of double-digit interest rates. This economic environment precipitated a shift from whole life to term insurance and UL insurance. Investment advisors encouraged their clients to "buy term and invest the rest." For many people, it made more sense to buy lower cost term insurance instead of whole life, and invest the "savings" in traditional investments. For others, purchasing UL insurance and "investing the rest" was an attractive alternative to whole life. Cash values were growing at 10% or more per year and UL was less expensive. Also, many insurance advisors found that UL was easier to sell than whole life because the UL sales illustrations displayed a lower initial premium cost.

Later, a new guaranteed version of UL was marketed by insurance carriers. Guaranteed universal life (GUL) insurance offers protection from dropping interest rates as long as the policy owner makes timely premium payments. Regardless of how much interest rates decline after the policy was sold, GUL policies are guaranteed to remain in force until termination (the death of the insured) even if the cash value of the policy goes to zero. Insurance advisors nicknamed these policies "term to age 100" because the lack of cash value makes them appear like level premium term policies that never lapse.

By the late 1990's, many carriers offered variable life insurance policies with the cash value tied to sub-accounts invested in stocks and bonds. Many agents peddled these policies using illustrations displaying rates of return of up to 12%. Later, hybrid policies that tied long-term care (LTC) benefits to the life insurance policies became popular. These policies offer to pay a portion of the death benefit while the insured is living in order to cover LTC expenses.

By 2008, several things became apparent regarding life insurance. Whole life insurance, considered a dinosaur product by the financial industry, became the best performing investment in the portfolios of many investors. Whole life performed as expected, and, in many cases, outperformed expectations because of the investment performance of the insurance companies. Investors who were reeling from a decline in their stock portfolios were happy to see that their whole life insurance increased its value.

Universal life (UL) insurance, however, became a disaster for many policy owners. These policies earned less than their illustrations suggested due to declining interest rates. This meant policy owners needed to increase their premiums in order to carry the policies to their life expectancies and beyond. Many older policy owners sold their UL policies to investors (life settlement) and reinvested the proceeds into GUL policies, guaranteed never to fail. Variable universal life insurance policies became poor investments, dropping in value with the decline of the stock market.

Throughout all this time the need for insurance has not changed. Insurance still builds an immediate estate. It can be used to guarantee loans, pay estate taxes, provide liquidity should a key person or partner die, equalize estates among children from separate marriages, provide money for charitable purposes, and fund buy-sell agreements.

What changed is the way life insurance is sold and the way investors view insurance. Many experienced life insurance agents are retiring, without younger agents to take their place. Many fee-only financial planners prefer not to advise clients about life insurance. Therefore, there are fewer professionals offering quality insurance advice.

Some wealthy investors have found that life insurance can also act as an investment, particularly if investors (often times strangers) pay their premiums. These investors view life insurance as a quick way to make money.

I believe investors need life insurance, but they are not necessarily receiving good insurance advice. Insurance products are complex, and sales illustrations used by agents may not reflect reality. With the "old school" of life agents retiring, the number of knowledgeable, experienced agents is declining. Many agents primarily represent one company, and are biased toward that company's products. Advisors who do not specialize in life insurance (stockbrokers, financial planners, etc.) do not understand how to "shop" large insurance policies to the carriers, and may be limited by their broker/dealers to working with a small number of products.

Investors need the help and expertise of professionals who understand insurance products and how they relate to financial, estate, and investment planning. In the new financial world of lower interest rates, deleveraging, a declining dollar, and an uncertain future, competent insurance advice is extremely important.

So what type of life insurance do you need? The answer depends on your needs, your current financial situation, your expected future financial situation, and the "who behind you." Below are three examples of how to creatively use insurance.

Mary and Long-Term Care Insurance

Mary lost her husband in a tragic car accident several years ago. The term life insurance on her husband's life provided enough money to educate their children and give her some savings. Mary is now in her late 50's. Her children graduated from college and found jobs. Mary is a "Financial Independent" who never wants to rely on her children for future assistance. She is working again and thinking about long-term care (LTC) insurance for herself. Mary has some minor medical issues that cannot be improved.

Rated LTC insurance, reflecting her medical condition, is very expensive. Those same medical issues also have a minor effect on her life insurance rating, which is "Standard" by several life insurance carriers. In Mary's situation, life insurance is less expensive than LTC but Mary does not view life insurance as a viable alternative to LTC insurance.

Mary has three options:

1. Purchase an expensive LTC policy that she may never need.

2. Purchase permanent life insurance (universal life) with the goal of providing a small "estate" for her children. Even if she has to spend her savings on long-term care in the future, the insurance "replaces" those funds and the proceeds pass to her children upon her death.

3. Purchase a "combination" insurance policy that combines life insurance and LTC benefits. Most combination insurance policies front a portion of the death benefit for long-term care purposes, if needed, with the remaining balance going to the insured's beneficiaries (the children in Mary's case). The premium is slightly higher than a standard universal life contract due to the LTC benefits combined in the policy.

Mary decides the combination policy is her best alternative. She is uncomfortable remaining uninsured, and it does not make sense for her to purchase expensive LTC insurance that may never be used. The second option is appealing but the third option is the best fit for Mary. She justifies the money she spends on the premiums with her primary desire to remain financially independent. She now has money available for long-term care. If the LTC benefits are not completely used, the life insurance will "replace" the assets Mary used to pay the premiums during her lifetime and provide some money for her children upon her death.

Wendy and Estate Equalization

Wendy has been married three times and has three teenage children from those marriages. She is currently married to Jim and they have two young children. Jim has no children from his previous marriage. Wendy and Jim have been married ten years, and it appears this marriage will last.

Wendy is financially successful in her own right (she made some money modeling before she met Jim and invested wisely) but not as wealthy as Jim who comes from a prominent East Coast "old money" family. Jim also made his own fortune in Silicon Valley. They do not have a pre-nuptial agreement, but there are various trusts in place to protect Jim's substantial assets as well as a private charitable foundation. Jim's father, John, died several months ago and left a substantial estate. Wendy was surprised to receive an eight-figure inheritance from him. John was very close with his son, Jim, and adored Wendy and all his grandchildren (including Wendy's teenagers from her previous marriages).

Wendy and Jim are both "Family Stewards" who believe the primary importance of wealth is taking care of their family. They are also altruistic and placed the bulk of the inheritance into trusts earmarked for charitable causes.

Jim has always been comfortable with money and understands the power and responsibility associated with great wealth. He has a strong work ethic, takes nothing for granted and continues to focus on success. Some of his family members have had trouble rising to the challenges and have not managed their lives and money responsibly. This has created much strife within the family, especially with his siblings.

Wendy feels that having "too much money" was the catalyst for many of the problems in her husband's family. She does not want that to happen in her family and is concerned that all of her children are treated equally (three from prior marriages and two with Jim).

Wendy's attorney found a simple solution to her concerns about estate equalization. He suggested the purchase of a $20 million life insurance policy on Wendy's life payable to the five children or their heirs. This way all her children would receive approximately the same amount of money upon her death. To keep the insurance proceeds outside of her estate, her attorney recommended that Wendy create an irrevocable life insurance trust for the benefit of her children. He also suggested the appointment of a corporate trustee for the administration of the trust. Rather than Wendy owning the policy individually, the trust would purchase and hold the policy.

The attorney and corporate trustee were interested in the best type of insurance to meet Wendy's needs. They reviewed various options and studied three of them in earnest. The first option, a popular strategy used by insurance consultants, combines three types of permanent insurance (whole life, universal life, and variable universal life insurance). Wendy and her advisors rejected this option because they did not want to risk paying a potentially higher premium should the equity markets perform worse than the projected variable universal life (VUL) illustrations suggested. They were also concerned that whole life would underperform relative to the historical illustrations, given the likelihood of lower interest rates.

The second option, a universal life (UL) insurance policy, was also rejected. Wendy and her advisors sought a guaranteed premium. The problem with universal life insurance is that investment performance may require higher premium payments at a later date.

The third option, a guaranteed universal life (GUL) policy, was chosen. GUL has several advantages, even though it will probably have no cash value after twenty years (per the illustration). The level premium was the least expensive of all the options. The premium was also guaranteed never to rise provided the trustee made timely payments to the carrier. Also, they believed insurance companies were mispricing these policies in the insured's favor. Interest rates have dropped since the liquidity crisis of 2008, and are likely to remain low for some time. Most insurance carriers have not taken this into consideration when pricing their policies. As a result, Wendy and her advisors felt a guaranteed premium made the most sense.

Frightened Fred and Frieda

Fred and Frieda are small business owners with enough cash flow to survive the current economic downturn. They are also "Financial Phobics" who do not like thinking about investments outside their business. What bothers them the most is the amount of savings they lost when the market dropped. They are looking for a simple and guaranteed "anchor" to their investment portfolio to ensure that they can sleep at night should another unexpected economic crisis occur. They are also interested in leaving an estate to their only son, who has been diagnosed with autism.

Fred and Frieda reviewed several investment and estate planning options. They decided to purchase tax deferred annuities and a $1 million whole life insurance policy because current interest rates are very low, and they expect inflation to rise later (hurting the value of long-term bonds).

Whole life, a "forgotten" insurance product, offers several benefits for them. The policy is guaranteed to endow with $1 million dollars in it. They have the option of borrowing against the cash value in the policy, if needed, to help their son while they are alive. Their son will receive a $1 million death benefit upon their death. While whole life is not an optimal choice for most people, it makes sense for "Financial Phobics" like Fred and Frieda.

From an estate planning perspective, they are concerned about protecting their son and providing for him after they are gone. Fred and Frieda have wills and other basic estate planning documents in place. Their attorney has recommended that they consider various trusts including a revocable living trust, an irrevocable life insurance trust and a special needs trust (supplemental needs trust).

CHAPTER 11

WHAT TO DO WITH YOUR
CURRENT LIFE INSURANCE

After the financial markets collapsed in 2008, many people were surprised that their whole life insurance became their best investment, earning in some cases close to 6% tax-free! Whole life policies (considered "dinosaurs" by most carriers who stopped marketing them years ago) are priced to endow at a certain age, usually age 100. An owner of a $1 million whole life policy is guaranteed to see the policy grow to at least its face amount ($1 million) should he or she live to age 100 and continue to pay the premiums.

But what about the majority of the investing public that own other forms of life insurance? What should they do? The answer lies with an expanded definition of life insurance. Life insurance in any form is more than a vehicle that provides funds at the death of the insured. It is also a capital asset that should be considered an investment. Similar to most capital assets, life insurance can be bought and sold in a secondary market. The potential to sell life insurance for a "fair market value" to a third party provides more options for policy owners but complicates the analysis of the asset.

Does viewing life insurance as a "capital asset" make it an investment? Most state insurance regulators dissuade agents and brokers from presenting or selling life insurance as an "investment." Regardless, many consumers consider life insurance as both a means of protection and a financial investment.

Before you decide what to do with your current life insurance, a thorough review and evaluation of your existing coverage is necessary. A "policy audit" by an independent, unbiased professional is the best way to determine if your life insurance is working optimally for you.

A thorough policy audit reviews and evaluates the following:

1. The financial strength of the carrier.

2. The face amount of the policy, to see if it still matches the potential liability.

3. The beneficiary designations.

4. The "performance" of the policy relative to the sales illustration.

5. The cost of new insurance vs. the cost of the current policy.

6. The viability of selling the current policy (if the insured is over 55) and using the proceeds to purchase new insurance at a lower premium.

7. The viability of selling the current policy (if the insured is over 55) and using the proceeds for any other purpose.

How often should you audit your insurance policies? Generally, your insurance needs should be reviewed whenever there are significant changes in your life or financial circumstances. Term insurance (temporary insurance) should be audited at least one year before coverage terminates at the end of the specified term. It should also be audited if you decide you no longer need or want the coverage and intend to let the policy lapse before the end of the term period. All forms of permanent insurance (whole life and various forms of universal life) should be reviewed every few years.

Policy audits are particularly beneficial for owners of universal life (UL) and variable universal life (VUL) insurance because many of these policies are now "failing." This is of great concern to those who view these types of permanent insurance as safe "investments." A "failing" life insurance policy is defined as a policy heading toward a certain lapse unless additional premium payments (usually at a higher rate) are made.

UL is an interesting form of insurance because it provides a tax-free build-up of the cash value and a tax-free death benefit (depending upon proper ownership structure and beneficiary designation). Many policy owners, trustees, and financial advisors believe that nothing can go wrong with a UL policy as long as the insurance carrier is financially stable. Nothing could be further from the truth. It turns out a lot of things can go wrong with a UL policy even if the insurance company remains financially sound. In fact, most of the life settlement business is being done with UL insurance policies

Why do UL policies fail? The reason has to do with the way they are sold. Life insurance is largely a commissioned product (no incentive to monitor the policy) typically sold by the agent who has the "best" illustrated premium. To the client, the "best" premium is usually the lowest one an agent or broker can legally display on a sales illustration. The problem with sales illustrations is that they are merely estimates and are not necessarily realistic projections of how a permanent policy will actually perform. For example, if interest rates are now lower than what was estimated on the original sales illustration, the policy will earn less than anticipated and increased premium payments will eventually become necessary to keep the policy in-force until maturity (the death of the insured). Generally, interest rates for highly rated fixed income securities have dropped since the 1980's, and fell significantly during and after the stock market crash of 2008. This means many UL policies are now heading toward certain failure unless the owners can make substantially higher premium payments.

Many variable universal life (VUL) insurance policies are also failing. ("Variable" refers to the investment component of this type of life insurance policy.) The reason VUL policies fail is similar to the reasons why UL policies fail, and has to do with the way VUL is marketed and sold. Agents and brokers can legally illustrate policy returns of "not greater than 12%," giving the impression that those returns are possible or even probable. When those optimistic assumptions are not realized, substantial additional premium payments are necessary to keep the policy from lapsing.

What steps should you take if you are holding a failing policy?

1. Determine if you still need the life insurance.

    Review why you purchased the life insurance and see if that need still exists. If the need has passed, or the life insurance is not entirely necessary, you may find you can do without it. Perhaps your estate is much smaller after the market crash and you do not need as much life insurance for estate planning purposes.

2. Write an insurance policy statement.

    If you still want or need the insurance, then you must write an "insurance policy statement." The insurance policy statement is similar to an investment policy statement (discussed in greater detail in the next chapter).

3. Obtain a "policy audit" and weigh all your options.

    An independent audit of your policy, performed by an unbiased third party, will help you weigh the relative advantages and disadvantages of keeping, selling, or lapsing the policy. The information you receive from the "policy audit" should help you decide which alternative is the best for you.

A perfect example is a corporation that owned a $2 million, 20-year term "Key-Man" insurance policy on the life of a departing executive. Since the policy was no longer needed, the corporation's initial decision was to let the policy lapse. An audit of the policy before it lapsed revealed that it was still convertible to a permanent policy, making it suitable for a life settlement. This eventually led to the policy being sold for $550,000. Any way you look at it, $550,000 is better than receiving $0 if the policy lapsed!

Another example is "Mary," an elderly widow with no immediate family, who was sold (inappropriately) an insurance policy she did not need. Her new financial advisor and her long-time attorney tried to get the insurance carrier to rescind the policy. The carrier refused. Rather than wait for an arbitration process that could take several years, she decided to sell the policy on the secondary market. The life settlement she obtained more than covered the cost of her investment in the life insurance.

Anyone interested in learning more about life insurance options can refer to my upcoming book, *Lies, Damn Lies, and Life Settlements,* which describes in detail the process of selling a policy. Since the end of 2008, the life settlement market has contracted because: (1) Deleveraging by investors caused a decline of investment funds; and (2) The lengthening of life expectancy assumptions used by the life settlement industry lowered the expected return by investors. This caused investors in life settlements to raise their required rates of return while simultaneously making it more beneficial for policy owners to keep their policies.

I am surprised that very few life insurance agents and brokers actively monitor and review the policies they have sold. I am more surprised that many trustees and other advisors do not monitor policies on a regular basis. I doubt much will change unless the industry stops paying the large up-front commissions on insurance products sold, giving agents and brokers no incentive to review their policies on an ongoing basis.

If you (or your business) currently own a life insurance policy, you should have it audited to see if it is "performing" as expected and then make any necessary changes. If you (or your business) have unnecessary, unwanted or failing life insurance, you should immediately have it audited and consider a life settlement as one of your options. Life insurance, even unwanted life insurance, is an important asset!

CHAPTER 12

THE INVESTMENT POLICY STATEMENT

The Investment Policy Statement (IPS) provides a framework for managing your portfolio. The IPS is a valuable tool for investors and advisors, and it should be a fundamental part of the documents governing your investment accounts.

While many investment firms and financial advisors recognize and understand the importance of a written IPS, it is often misused. Most firms and advisors use a computerized program that creates an IPS designed to funnel their clients' funds into a previously designated financial product. This product is usually a "wrap account or platform," which involves the typical asset allocation among various mutual funds or separate account managers. The IPS serves as a conduit into a financial product rather than a customized document tailored to the investor.

I believe every high net worth investor deserves an IPS that is customized according to his or her needs and objectives. I also believe that clients should not automatically have their funds directed into a "one size fits all" financial product.

What are the advantages of a custom IPS?

1. It summarizes your personal goals and desires, not those of anyone else. This includes your individual goals as well as your objectives for your business, trust accounts, and other entities. A separate IPS may be written for each type

of account as necessary.

2. It keeps your investment advisor "on the same page" as you.

3. It is easy for you and others to understand. For example, you may wish to share the information with family members, other financial advisors, legal counsel, etc.

4. It can provide continuity in the event something happens to your current investment advisor (retirement, death, disability, etc.) or if you change advisors. Another competent investment advisor can immediately understand how to manage your account.

How do you create an IPS? Writing an IPS should not be a daunting or difficult task. You can use the outline below as a guide. The format does not matter as long as it covers all areas relevant to the particular account. The content will vary depending on the type and purpose of the account. Generally, the following areas should be included in an IPS:

1. Overview/Purpose of the Account

2. Investment Objectives

3. Risk Tolerance

4. Return Criteria

5. Tax Issues

6. Timing of Distributions

7. Legal Issues

8. Liquidity Issues

9. Unique Preferences

10. Investment Strategy

11. Process for Choosing Investments

12. Selection Criteria for Investment Managers

13. Monitoring and Rebalancing

My test of a good IPS requires a "yes" answer to the following:

1. Does the client fully understand and agree with all aspects of the IPS?

2. Was most of the IPS written before the investment strategy was developed (i.e., the IPS is not a computerized conduit into an asset allocation platform)?

3. Is the IPS simple enough for most of it to fit on one page in a bullet point format?

4. Can the client's other advisors (attorney, CPA, trust officer, etc.) look at the IPS and quickly and easily understand how the account is managed?

5. If anything should happen to the primary advisor, can another competent advisor read the IPS and immediately understand how to manage/oversee the account?

High net worth investors who demand custom investment solutions must have custom, and not product specific, investment policy statements. A customized statement, in the hands of a skilled advisor, can lead to a variety of investment solutions for high net worth investors and take into account the prevailing and expected social, economic, and political conditions.

CHAPTER 13

EXAMPLES

Dave the Doctor

Dave, 63, is a married anesthesiologist with two children who are now working. He is a partner in a large practice with other doctors and earns approximately $450,000 per year. He and his wife, Dianne, 59, have no trouble spending their earned income money and enjoy living the good life. Unfortunately, they lost significant money using financial advisors who placed a large portion of Dave's portfolio in technology stocks before 2000. They also lost money after their financial assets were asset allocated in a purportedly "safe" manner before 2008. Needless to say, Dave does not fully trust financial advisors!

Dave and Dianne need around $12,000 per month to cover their "Basic Needs." An expected inheritance from Dave's family will cover any remaining mortgages on their two homes. They have $1.9 million in retirement assets and no outstanding debt except for the mortgages.

Dave and his wife are not expecting to divorce, they have reasonable health and disability insurance, and they want to invest wisely. Dave intends to retire in five years and sell his portion of the practice (to his partners) for $700,000. What should Dave and Dianne do?

First, Dave and Dianne must discover their personality types, or "who" they really are. Dave is a cross between a "Financial Phobic" (who finds it difficult to think about money and investing) and a "Family Steward" (who wants to ensure his estate is set up properly to benefit his spouse, children, grandchildren, and charities, in that order). Dianne is a "VIP" and "Family Steward," meaning wealth is first about enjoyment and image, and then about benefiting her family.

It is important for Dave and Dianne to understand their financial personalities so they know how they got to their current financial condition, why they made previous mistakes, and what they must do to be content in the future. For example, Dianne's insistence on buying a home near the "best" school in their city helped their home retain value when local real estate crashed. Her choice to go with "top advisors," based solely on the assumption that they were financially successful, combined with Dave's apathy toward investing, hurt them financially.

Once Dave and Dianne understand who they are, they must decide how they want to live the remainder of their lives and quantify what is needed to do so. Then they need to explore what to do with their remaining estate (after death), and find optimal strategies to ensure their wishes are met.

Dave and Dianne's financial and investment desires are relatively simple and fit nicely into the three categories described in the earlier chapters of this book: (1) Basic Needs; (2) Wants, Wishes & Desires (things they like to do); and (3) Legacy or Estate Planning.

It turns out that their "Basic Needs" are greater in retirement than what most people require in pre-retirement years. Their lifestyle is a good one, and they do not want to change it. In addition, they desire long-term care insurance that is relatively expensive today (it will not get any cheaper) and consider this a basic need. Dave and Dianne have already accumulated enough in retirement and other funds for their basic needs to be covered by safe and guaranteed investments.

They should invest their other assets for the future, taking into consideration the prevailing social, economic, and political conditions (something many promoters of "asset allocation" do not do). They "have enough" to cover their "Basic Needs" as well as their "Wants, Wishes & Desires" or "Non-Basic Needs" (the things they like to do). Therefore, logic dictates that taking an investment risk that could lead to a large loss is something that should be avoided at all costs. Their "Non-Basic Needs" assets should be very well diversified, with an emphasis on income producing securities backed by stable or growing cash flow from operations (less risk). These can be from both taxable and tax-efficient investments. Stocks, inflation protected bonds, dividend producing common stocks, closed-end funds selling at large discounts to their net asset value (NAV), and other vehicles should be examined for inclusion in their portfolio.

Asset-liability matching is a reasonable strategy Dave and Dianne can use in several areas of their portfolio, provided they can accept the risk. One example is energy. Dave and Dianne live in the Northeast, and their heating/air conditioning bills average $750 per month between their two homes. They can buy a basket of energy stocks and/or publicly traded partnerships (through closed-end funds, exchange traded funds, or individual issues) that will provide them with the income they need to cover energy costs. The income from their investments will rise when the economy improves (and someday it will) and energy costs rise. The danger or risk is if energy prices decline even more, then the value of their investment drops. Either way, Dave and Dianne will have assets that should reasonably match the volatile liability of their energy costs (provided they are comfortable with this strategy).

After taking care of their "Basic Needs" and "Non-Basic Needs," they should focus on the third layer—their "Legacy"—estate and gift planning strategies. Their charitable and estate planning goals are relatively simple. They want to provide for their family and make gifts to various charities that are important to them.

Dianne is a longstanding board member of an international charitable organization and Dave is active in a local religious organization. They want to continue making current contributions to Dianne's charity and leave money to Dave's charity after his death. To accomplish some of their charitable goals as well as provide for their heirs, they are exploring the use of various trusts and life insurance as part of their overall estate plan.

One option they are considering is a Charitable Lead Trust for the purpose of making gifts to Dianne's charity during her lifetime with the remaining amount in the trust going to their children and grandchildren after her death. Besides fulfilling some of their charitable giving goals and commitments, this type of trust provides estate and gift tax benefits that may be advantageous to Dave and Dianne.

Another option is a Charitable Remainder Trust. This type of trust would provide a stream of income to Dave and Dianne during their lifetimes and benefit their favorite charity, charities or a Family Foundation upon their deaths. Dave and Dianne are interested in creating a Family Foundation to encourage their children and grandchildren to become more involved in philanthropic pursuits. They are also considering an Irrevocable Life Insurance Trust for the benefit of their family. If they establish a Charitable Remainder Trust, the Life Insurance Trust would "replace" some of the wealth that is going to charity. This strategy may also provide Dave and Dianne with certain income tax benefits, and estate and gift tax advantages.

Insurance can also play a role in charitable giving and estate planning. Permanent insurance is a special financial tool because it can come with guarantees not found in other investments. It is also one of the ways that Dave has decided to contribute to his charity. The religious organization is the owner and beneficiary of a guaranteed premium universal life insurance policy on Dave's life that will never lapse. During his lifetime, Dave has arranged to make gifts to the charity to cover the annual premium payments. The charity will receive the proceeds of the policy when he dies.

In addition to the insurance policy that will ultimately benefit charity, Dave previously purchased a large life insurance policy for estate protection. Part of the rationale for this policy is to protect his assets from potential lawsuits due to unfavorable liability laws in the state where he practices. Thanks to a life insurance policy audit, Dave discovered the policy is heading for failure/lapse when he turns 78 years old unless substantially more premium payments are made. He has several options including: making additional payments now to keep the policy going; selling the policy near age 78 (when a successful life settlement is more likely) and buying a new policy with the proceeds; or seeking a reduced, paid-up option after retirement. Dave and Dianne can defer this decision to a later date, but they should monitor the policy carefully on a regular basis to see if it begins to fail at a faster rate.

Dave and Dianne will be much happier managing their assets by following this three-layer approach instead of relying on traditional asset allocation. The multi-tiered or multi-layered investment approach is a better way to manage money because it relies on common sense and prudent investment analysis.

Roger and Rhonda the Retired Couple

Rhonda and Roger retired seven years ago after buying a modest home (no mortgage) in a sunny and warm state. Their kids are grown and do not need financial assistance. Rhonda and Roger have several grandchildren whom they enjoy "spoiling" during the holidays. They found a financial advisor who guided them into a typical asset allocation investment program. Their investments were allocated assuming an expected return of 8%. The market crash destroyed 25% of their portfolio, and they do not know what to do now.

Rhonda and Roger are "Financial Independents" who never want to be a burden to their children and would prefer not to seek any financial assistance from them. Rhonda and Roger are in good health and proud to live independently. They enjoy life and wish to spend their remaining years enjoying social activities, golf, tennis, traveling, and visiting their children and grandchildren. They have few charitable interests now that their volunteer years are over. They expect their remaining estate will go to their children. Unfortunately, there is not enough cash flow from their portfolio and retirement accounts to fund their desired lifestyle.

The best way to approach their situation is to use the multi-layered investment framework to help them define their various goals and objectives for each layer—"Basic Needs," "Wants, Wishes & Desires" (things they like to do), "Legacy Planning" —and then match appropriate investment strategies to those layers. Rhonda and Roger acknowledged that the standard asset allocation strategy would not work for them. They opted for the customized investment approach combined with common sense to match appropriate strategies to each layer and take advantage of the best available investments at the time.

While analyzing their other expenses (not Basic Needs), they realized that they needed to spend less on social activities (e.g., a country club membership) and limit overseas travel expenditures. Since most of their social life revolves around their club, they decided to travel less overseas and reposition their portfolio to add income. One way to cover these expenses, including the country club cost, is through asset-liability matching using higher distributing individual securities and closed-end funds selling at large discounts to net asset value. These are riskier investments, but they are relatively safe (compared to what they had) because of the high distribution rates and large discounts that should close over time. Part of Rhonda and Roger's portfolio should be placed in investments that are expected to grow over time, assuming the world eventually rebounds from the current financial crisis. Their potential long-term care liabilities can be covered through an innovative life insurance policy that forwards the death benefit (should long-term care needs arise) with the unused portion going to their heirs. This allows them to remain independent and potentially leave an estate to their heirs.

The traditional asset allocation strategy is not appropriate for this couple. Their time horizon is not unlimited and they never want to become dependent upon their children. Rhonda and Roger cannot tolerate more losses because they probably do not have time for the markets to return to previous levels. An innovative solution was found by weighing various options (so they do not have to curtail all of their social and travel activities) and using a customized, common sense investment approach.

CHAPTER 14

DELEVERAGING AND WHY
P/E RATIOS MUST FALL

Since late 2008, we have all been hearing a lot about the term "deleveraging," yet some investors and their financial advisors do not fully understand it or realize the short and long range implications deleveraging has on their portfolios. I believe deleveraging will permanently change the way many securities are valued. This means the equity return assumptions used by most advisors using asset allocation models are wrong and will lead to disappointed investors. Understanding the impact of deleveraging is imperative to estimating future equity returns and estimating how to allocate investor portfolios.

"Deleveraging" is simply the unwinding of "leverage." In the financial world, leverage refers to borrowing money to purchase assets. Corporations lever their investments because they believe the returns they receive on their borrowed assets will exceed their carrying costs (debt). For example, a Wall Street brokerage may borrow $3 billion from investors by issuing bonds at 9% and then use the funds to purchase an asset expected to earn them 14% or more per year. The firm borrowed $3 billion but expects to immediately add $150 million per year to its cash flow.

Leverage among Wall Street firms grew dramatically in the decade preceding 2008 for two very good reasons: greed and insurance. Greed meant more bonuses, and on Wall Street that meant billions of dollars paid out to employees (some Wall Street participants earn over $1 billion per year). Institutions did whatever they could to increase profits because a percentage of those profits lined the pockets of the employees and partners responsible for them. Insurance was the catalyst that sparked the leverage. With newly created derivative investments called "credit default swaps," companies could leverage even greater amounts of their capital, believing that their potential losses were limited (insured against loss).

In early 2008, billionaire investor George Soros pounded the table (figuratively), warning us how out of control leverage could create an imminent financial disaster. He was, as usual, correct. Warren Buffett, one of the world's wealthiest men, spoke of a potential disaster created by derivative investments. Eventually, Soros, Buffett, economist Gary Shilling, and others who warned about an impending financial disaster were proven correct. Venerable Wall Street institutions like Merrill Lynch, AIG, Bear Stearns, and Lehman Brothers either went belly-up or were nearly ruined because they could not deleverage quickly enough.

After the crash of 2008, the media reported extensively about corporations reducing their leverage. For example, in December, 2008, Morgan Stanley reported that it intended to reduce its leverage from over 30 times capital to a mere 15 times capital! But what happens to earnings and cash flow when leverage is decreased, and what does that do to your equity returns?

Deleveraging occurs when assets are sold to reduce debt (the money borrowed). If we assume that the assets generated more cash flow than the carrying cost of the debt (debt service), then cash flow is reduced when these assets are sold. Lower cash flow reduces the chance of improving future earnings and distributions (dividends). This leads to lower prices because securities are priced by discounting future cash flows and dividends. Wall Street typically "pays up" for faster growing companies, and they typically sell for higher P/E ratios than companies that grow more slowly. Therefore, deleveraging leads to both lower absolute earnings and lower P/E ratios.

Should you invest in stocks now that we know why the P/E ratios of individual stocks (and individual stocks make up "the market") are not likely to stay at the high double-digit levels of the past few decades? The answer is yes, you should absolutely invest some money in equities, provided you do not invest the way you have in the past.

The deleveraging we are experiencing today will last for a long time. Deleveraging has far-reaching implications for all financial markets. It will certainly change the way equities are valued since deleveraged companies will have less future cash flow. In the long run, I believe equities will sell for lower P/E ratios than they did in the past. As a result, I believe now is the time for investors to eschew passively managed strategies and to invest in stocks with superior risk-return potential.

CHAPTER 15

A NEW LOOK AT PROFESSIONALLY MANAGED INVESTMENTS

Most investors do not have the time, interest or expertise to competently analyze securities or portfolio managers. This simple fact has resulted in "professionally managed investments" for individuals and institutions. These types of investments are overseen by a (presumably) competent portfolio manager or team of managers and analysts who are dedicated to the day-to-day management of a defined group of securities for the investing public or institutions. Professionally managed accounts take several forms. The first type is an account that "pools" capital from many investors. Examples include mutual funds and exchange traded funds. The second form is a separately managed account that is usually available only to high net worth investors, although a small investor form of it has appeared in recent years. A third form involves investments that are not "liquid," referring to their inability to be readily sold to a willing buyer at a fair price. Examples include many partnerships in real estate, commodities and private equity.

Open-End Mutual Funds

Open-end mutual funds are a time honored investment vehicle

going back to 1928 (in America), and are the most popular investment vehicle of the last two decades for individual investors. A professionally managed mutual fund pools money from many investors and invests that money in various securities in accordance with the fund's objective. These funds offer daily pricing at the net asset value of the assets (minus fees) and daily liquidity. The fund sponsor receives revenue by charging fees for portfolio management, legal, accounting, and auditing costs. Net income and net realized gains (short and long-term capital gains) are generally "passed through" to the shareholders of the mutual fund and taxed at the individual investor's rates.

Mutual funds can be specific or general in their stated investment goals. One mutual fund may, for example, specialize in Asian real estate, while another looks for small-cap value stocks worldwide. Most funds stick to their stated investment goals, although their internal process may change over time. The professional management of most mutual funds did not protect the investors in the market crash of 2008 since most funds stay fully invested and do not hedge or have a "portfolio insurance" policy.

Most open-end mutual funds booked large losses in 2008 giving their investors an important tax advantage called "loss carryforwards," a special tax treatment based upon Generally Accepted Accounting Principles (GAAP). A tax loss carryforward is an accounting technique that reduces tax liability by applying net operating losses to future years' profits. This means you can invest in many mutual funds and not pay capital gains taxes for up to 7 years following the year the loss was incurred! Mutual fund "loss carryforwards" are a big advantage for many post-2008 investors.

While this opportunity for tax-free gains is almost too good to ignore, mutual funds do have some disadvantages: (1) Management fees are sometimes higher than alternative methods of investing; (2) Most active managers do not beat their relevant index; (3) Many funds are sold with sales charges (loads); and

(4) Mutual funds do not offer the customized buying and selling of individual securities.

Open-end mutual funds may not be your first choice for future investments, though, the potential to avoid paying tax on future gains, because of the embedded post-2008 loss carryforwards in many of these funds, can be very attractive to investors.

Closed-End Mutual Funds

Closed-end mutual funds are similar to open-end funds except for two major things: (1) The price is determined similar to a stock based upon the market, and not solely upon the net asset value of the fund; and (2) The number of shares remains constant. Closed-end funds can sell at a "premium" or "discount" to their net asset value (the value of the underlying securities).

After the 2008 crash, there were many mutual funds selling at 30 percent discounts to their net asset value (NAV)! Today, some funds are still selling at high discounts, though the percentage discount has narrowed. For example, some closed-end bond funds are still selling at 10 percent or greater discounts to their NAV. The discount to NAV makes the yield relatively higher than an open-end fund owning the same securities. Closed-end bond funds also offer the potential for greater gains.

In recent years, Wall Street underwrote a plethora of closed-end funds. Many of these funds are in specialty areas allowing investors to immediately and cheaply change their investment strategy. For example, for the mere cost of a discounted stock trade, you can use closed-end funds to add or short a position in: foreign real estate; stocks representing a particular commodity; foreign or domestic stock markets; and any sector of the fixed income market.

Investors should almost never purchase a closed-end fund as a new issue because it is almost a certainty that these funds will eventually go to a discount, offering investors a better opportunity to purchase them. As with open-end funds, do your own research and due diligence (consider the risks, objectives, fees and expenses) before investing. It is important to look at the portfolio management team and understand their investment process. Also, you should analyze the total internal management fees, and legal, accounting and auditing expenses.

Closed-end funds are required to pay out their short and long-term gains and losses similar to open-end funds. Loss carryforwards also exist in these funds, and that is very important to knowledgeable investors.

Most financial advisors utilize open-end funds as investments, but I find that closed-end funds offer some advantages over their open-end counterparts. Unlike an open-end fund, closed-end managers do not have incentives to "market" to get more investors into the fund since the number of shares of a closed-end fund is fixed. These managers can concentrate on managing their portfolio, which is what you want them to do. Closed-end funds have no sales charges associated with buying them after the initial offering and have no penalties for selling them. The cost to buy or sell them is the cost of buying or selling a stock. Some closed-end funds have lower total costs than similar open-end funds. Closed-end funds selling at a discount to NAV often have significantly higher yields than open-end funds with similar investments.

If closed-end funds are often the better investment choice, why are open-end funds more popular? Part of the reason is tradition. The investing public and financial advisors are used to selling open-end funds. Part of the reason is fear. Many advisors consider closed-end funds a "stock." These advisors do not wish to buy and sell stocks in a client's portfolio. Part of the reason is greed. Loaded open-end funds pay high commissions to financial advisors who work on a commission basis. Closed-end funds (not newly issued) are bought and sold like stocks and the trading commissions are small. Part of the reason is licensure. Many financial advisors are salespeople licensed for mutual funds and insurance. They do not hold a FINRA Series 7 license necessary to buy and sell stocks.

Closed-end funds have advantages over other forms of investments, and should be considered for investments for individuals in their post-2008 portfolios.

Separate Account Management

There are two types of separate account management (SAM). The first is for the wealthy and/or institutional client and is characterized by high minimum investments with individually managed portfolios. For example, a manager with a long-short investment strategy may require a minimum investment of $25 million.

The second type of separate account management is for the masses. This form has a much lower minimum investment, usually $100,000. These investments are sometimes sold directly to the public, but are usually sold inside "wrap platforms" consisting of many other SAMs. These investments have strategies that are similar to mutual funds, so larger minimum investments are not necessary for the manager to competently do his job.

In the last 15 years, stockbrokers and other financial advisors have come to appreciate the benefits of SAM platforms and are comfortable offering these programs to their clients. SAM platforms provide an excellent array of investment management products, make financial reporting easy, and can be used as "style" proxies for an advisor's asset allocation model. These platforms allow the advisor to charge a yearly fee for ostensibly reviewing and monitoring the various investment managers in the program (how well they do this is debatable). Usually, it is the advisor's broker/dealer or firm that approves the managers in each wrap platform and then reviews the managers' performance and adherence to the stated investment policy.

Most separate account managers manage money in a narrowly defined fashion. This means a "large capitalization growth manager" invests mostly in large capitalization growth stocks and judges his or her performance on a relative basis to a pre-determined benchmark. Their job is usually not to raise cash to protect the portfolio against a market crash. Therefore, separate account managers generally did not protect investors during the market crash of 2008 because it was not their responsibility to do so. For tax purposes, the individual investor directly owns the "separate account" as of the date of investment in the account, similar to an investor purchasing individual securities. Therefore, you cannot use the tax losses attributed to previous investors as you could in an open-ended mutual fund.

Advantages of separate account managers include obtaining specialty investment management from managers who, in theory, are working directly for you. Also, fees are often less than those for other forms of investments.

Separate account managers are both more and less useful for individual investors in the post-2008 market crash environment. For the truly wealthy, SAMs represent a great way to have access to great investment strategies from top managers. For the masses, they simply offer another proxy to asset allocation, and we know asset allocation did not work well for the past decade!

Illiquid Investments

Investments that can be bought and sold readily are called "liquid." Examples include individual securities and mutual funds. Investments that cannot be readily bought and sold are considered "illiquid." It may take time to find a buyer to pay a fair price for an illiquid investment. Managed illiquid investments mostly consist of some form of partnership. Investments in currency, commodities, hedge strategies, and real estate are sometimes done through a partnership.

The recent market crash and corresponding loss of some $4 trillion of global wealth did present some unusual opportunities in illiquid investments. Some of these investments must be sold by people with cash flow problems, yet they have no ready market. This means you can find some nifty bargains in the secondary market for partnerships or through private deals. As always, do your investment and legal research first.

Exchange Traded Funds

The largest growth in managed investments has come from exchange traded funds, which are essentially passively managed index funds allowing investors to buy or sell an entire portfolio of securities in a single, inexpensive transaction. An exchange traded fund (ETF) can own general indexes (owning or tracking "the market") or specific investments, depending upon its charter. For the cost of buying or selling a stock, ETFs allow portfolio managers and individual investors to gain or reduce exposure to everything from Asian real estate to an index of commodities.

The price of an ETF, similar to the price of a closed-end fund, is determined by supply and demand. Unlike closed-end funds, institutional investors are allowed to redeem 50,000 shares in-kind when there is a gap between the market price and the NAV of an ETF. This arbitrage makes it highly unusual for an ETF to trade at a significant premium or discount.

ETFs have several advantages over mutual funds and separate accounts. ETF management fees are generally much less expensive than other types of managed investments. They offer a quicker (almost instantaneous) way to immediately gain exposure to specific areas of the markets. ETFs also make it easy for investors to asset-liability match, hedge their portfolios or speculate. For example, an investor may think the Federal Reserve's response to the current financial crisis will be eventually become inflationary. He can partially protect the value of his long-term bonds by purchasing a suitable amount of TBT, which is a double-inverse ETF of the 20-year Treasury bond.

One disadvantage of ETFs is the lack of tax loss carry-forwards. Another disadvantage is with market tracking. ETFs should, at least in theory, go up and down in proportion to their relevant index. In practice, some do not. The double-inverse 20-year treasury ETF mentioned above is a perfect example. The fund resets its pricing on a daily basis, which means it will never track the underlying 20-year bond perfectly. The biggest disadvantage of an ETF is the lack of active management. In a bull market, many active managers with good security selection skills taking average risk fail to beat the market because their return is reduced substantially by management fees and expenses. In an uneven market, managers with positive security selection skills tend to outperform by a greater margin.

CHAPTER 16

FINANCIAL ADVISORS

I have extensive technical and practical experience working with investment managers, financial institutions (broker/dealers, banks), financial advisors, and clients. My 30-plus years in the financial services industry has given me an "insider's perspective" of the investment advisory process. My first career, before consulting to clients about their wealth, was working for investment managers for nearly a quarter of a century. I was privileged to meet and work with some of the top managers in the industry and gained invaluable insight into how managers think and how they approach the markets. During this period, I marketed and sold investment products and funds to financial advisors and often provided consultations to some of their top clients. I gave technical presentations to advisors, CPAs, trust officers, and attorneys, and was invited to speak at numerous prestigious industry events. At these events, I met with some of the "crème de la crème" of advisors, many of whom became quite wealthy.

I met over 3000 stockbrokers, financial planners, and bankers during that phase of my life. Of those advisors, I would characterize maybe 60 (that's only 2%!) as being real investment "thinkers," that is, advisors who were capable of custom designing a portfolio for each client. I considered the other 98% to be "product salespersons," or advisors who tended to take a "one product fits all" approach to investing each client's assets.

Examples of product salespersons are advisors who place almost every client into the same mutual fund group or wrap platform regardless of the individual needs of each client. There is nothing wrong with product salespersons per se. Many have a history of consistently improving the financial well-being of their clients. But recognize that the advice they give is not customized.

Product salespersons can earn their income by charging fees, accepting commissions, or a combination of the two. Some product salespersons are expert at financial planning. Some have experts at their disposal who handle their clients' financial planning concerns.

After reading the previous chapters of this book, you might erroneously assume that I dislike most financial advisors. As in any profession, there are all kinds of people—those who will exceed your expectations, those who will meet your expectations, and those who will fail to meet them. The idea, of course, is to find people who consistently meet or exceed your expectations! Unfortunately, the financial advisory industry is filled with advisors who fail to meet expectations because of their erroneous belief and blind faith in asset allocation. These are advisors who see asset allocation as the end-all solution for their clients' investment strategies.

The advisors I like are ethical, competent, diligent, intelligent, and able to think outside of the asset allocation box. This kind of thinking allows them to find optimal, customized solutions for their clients' needs based upon current market conditions (as opposed to "asset allocating" every dime of their clients' assets). They exist to help and provide excellent service to their clients, and the money they earn is simply a byproduct of doing so.

Some of these advisors are not engaged in "financial planning." They have particular areas of expertise that do not require a general knowledge of the financial planning process. I assume that you, the reader of this book, already agree with me that financial planning and investment management are two different things. As a result, you are seeking more than one advisor. Below are some examples of different types of financial and investment advisors and the clients they are best suited for.

Marcy the Fee-Only Planner

Marcy is a "touchy-feely" independent advisor who builds trust with her clients by getting to know them well and treating them like members of her family. She believes in the financial planning process, and writes a financial plan for every client. Marcy has some wealthy clients but most of her income stream comes from her upper middle class clients. Early in her career, she made some investment mistakes. Surprisingly, no one complained, and she did not lose any of her clients (bull markets tend to make all advisors look brilliant). Marcy is now highly competent in all aspects of her practice. She writes a custom investment policy statement for each investment account. Almost all of her clients' assets are placed in wrap platforms and/or in quality, low-cost managed investments.

Marcy has a business model that consists of spending the most time possible with clients (this eventually leads to quality referrals), and delegating all other functions to industry experts. She delegates the writing of financial plans to another CFP® and then reviews and edits the plans before giving them to clients. All insurance-based needs are outsourced to knowledgeable and trusted insurance agents. Individual stock and bond analysis is delegated to trusted specialists.

Marcy's clientele consists of the very people for whom she is best suited. These are people who do not like making decisions, who need help in making decisions, and who require someone knowledgeable to call upon on a regular basis.

The "Marcys" of the financial planning world are wonderful for clients who need financial planning advice and prefer mostly managed investments. They are not the right planners for people who are looking for cutting-edge ideas or individual securities management. They are also not a good fit for investors who want prestigious institutions to manage their money.

Carl the Broker

Carl was a former "All Star" fixed income portfolio manager who got tired of a younger boss asking him to put more risk in his portfolio. He had already earned enough money to retire when he called his boss an idiot (I am being polite) and quit to do what he always wanted to do: help individual investors.

At first, Carl seemed like a "fish out of water" working as a "financial consultant" in the retail division of a large wirehouse. The idea of doing anything for the sake of earning a higher commission was foreign to him. After one frustrating year, he found a niche market of investors who could appreciate his investing knowledge and acumen. He is now a "large producer" who is left alone by his branch manager.

Carl's clients are mostly wealthy individuals who need help designing prudently managed fixed income portfolios. Carl is an expert in the fixed income markets and knows how to take advantage of prevailing market conditions. His largest referral came from a man who profited greatly from Carl's suggestion to sell most of his portfolio for a tax loss and immediately reposition the funds in closed-end funds selling at historic discounts. Carl refers estate planning, insurance, and other matters to others within his firm. He has no idea how well his firm handles these matters.

Carl is perfect for clients within his area of expertise. While many of his clients appreciate him, I doubt that they fully understand how his fixed income knowledge adds value to their portfolios.

Jerry the Dinosaur

Jerry is the "dinosaur" in his large brokerage, having spent the past 30 years buying stocks and bonds for his clients based upon the recommendations of his firm's best analyst. Jerry is a "survivor" because he can intuitively figure out what makes a security a good value.

Most of Jerry's clients are getting older and occasionally they ask about estate planning or gifting assets. He refers this business to other associates in his office who are knowledgeable in these areas.

I believe the "Jerrys" of the world are useful for finding the occasional great investment idea and for helping clients to structure basic equity and fixed income portfolios. The weaknesses of these "dinosaurs" are obvious. They are not for people with estate planning, insurance, and trust concerns. Nor are they for people who seek a "set it and forget it" portfolio.

Ben the Insurance Agent

Ben is an agent for a large insurance carrier. He is an experienced "big producer" who sells a lot of his firm's products. Therefore, his firm does not mind too much when he remains "honest" by showing competitor's products to his clients. Ben understands the ins and outs of life insurance, particularly how it is used within the estate planning process. When Ben acts as a broker, the client's interests are always placed ahead of his own. He rarely sees his clients after his sales, but does follow the "performance" of the multi-million dollar policies he sells. Clients can expect him to call if changes in premiums are necessary.

Great insurance professionals are hard to find. I believe most life insurance agents and brokers have no idea how to "manage" and underwrite a large insurance case. Most agents and brokers are not aware of how to "audit" life insurance and get the most out of it. When it comes to insurance, finding an expert who knows the tricks of the trade is valuable.

Ben, like most dedicated insurance agents, should be avoided for investment, financial planning, or overall estate planning advice, since he is predisposed to view insurance as the best solution for most financial needs.

Alexandra the Trust Officer

Alexandra is a private banker/advisor for one of the largest financial institutions in the world. Her background includes graduating from an Ivy League law school and working as a trust and investment officer at a prestigious trust company. She has expertise in estate planning for the ultra high net worth individuals along with extensive knowledge of investment management. She works with her clients' tax and legal advisors to ensure that her clients' needs and objectives are addressed. Her firm offers both individual investment management (subject to committee approval) and asset allocation through approved investment managers. Alexandra's firm earns more money from having hundreds of billions of dollars under management in investment management, trust and estate accounts than from charging fees for financial planning services.

I find most ultra high net worth individuals and families need trust services for estate planning, charitable planning, and generational planning purposes. Some of the wealthy use individual trustees, often a trusted CPA or financial advisor. Many prefer corporate fiduciaries and the security of knowing that the bank or trust company will always be there to provide continuity of management. Bank trust companies typically have legal and accounting professionals in-house and are held to a higher legal and fiduciary standard than an individual trustee. Alexandra is the right advisor for those clients who desire "special" treatment and expect to pay for it. Her firm has well-dressed professionals who work overtime to provide their clients with private banking, trust, investment, and philanthropic planning services.

Alexandra and her company are unlikely to provide truly customized investment advice, since most bank trust companies are, at least in my opinion, overly concerned with managing accounts "prudently," and avoiding any legal problems regarding investment performance.

Steve the Financial Planner

Steve is a CERTIFIED FINANCIAL PLANNER™ practitioner who has earned the Chartered Financial Analyst (CFA) designation. As a CFP® professional and a CFA charterholder, he understands financial planning, and investment strategy and analysis. Steve has been practicing for over twenty years and has learned to do things one way: his way. He once had a "business" with three other planners working for him. He discovered that the "business" stopped listening to clients and simply "rubber stamped" all clients' assets into the same asset allocation investments. Horrified, he separated from his other planners and went back to a single-person practice offering custom investment advice. Steve now has limited his practice to 100 clients and "upgrades" them periodically based upon profitability. Clients who are no longer in his "Top 100" are referred to another local planner who Steve deems competent.

Steve is a great financial advisor for most people reading this book, if they have enough assets to fit into his 100-person clientele. He provides clients with the financial planning they need and gives them adequate attention. He also designs and implements a tailor-made investment strategy for each of his clients. The two concerns about working with Steve are: (1) The size of the account you have to maintain to fit his "Top 100" business model; and (2) The lack of continuity in his financial advisory practice (should something happen to Steve).

The Big Broker Team

Tom, Dick, and Harry, successful stockbrokers at a wirehouse, established a partnership. With each partner specializing in a different function of the practice (prospecting, portfolio management, and client service), the team was able to spend more time working with top clients. The partners primarily manage portfolios using an in-house asset allocation model. Managed accounts are the preferred investment vehicle in lieu of mutual funds. Most clients are charged 1% for this service. The partners buy some individual securities for their accounts using in-house research. They use their in-house experts for estate planning and trust services.

The partners are operating the preferred business model for wirehouses. Their objectives are to give good financial advice to clients and increase assets under management. This model works well for many high net worth clients who do not need a completely customized approach to managing their money. The disadvantages are the fees charged to clients (assuming their employer does not allow the team to discount their services), and the inability to completely customize a portfolio because of the in-house bureaucracy inherent in large organizations.

Fran the Family Office President

Fran heads a multi-family office offering multi-generational estate planning and investment services to a handful of wealthy families. Family offices are designed to serve the financial and organizational needs of one or more extremely wealthy families. Fran and her staff do everything – interviewing and hiring investment managers, organizing the use of the office's private jet, helping the families with their charitable inclinations, and arranging for the best re-hab center for one of the grandchildren.

The family office is the ultimate advisory model for extremely wealthy families in search of a customized approach for managing their wealth, organizing their lives, and gifting their assets. If your net worth is large enough (probably over $50 million), starting a family office may be a good idea.

The above are a sampling of financial advisors I have met throughout my 30 years in the financial service industry. There are many, many more. Somewhere out there is the right one for you.

CHAPTER 17

WHAT TO DO NOW

How should you proceed if you agree with the ideas presented in this book? First, be realistic and do not deny what happened in 2008. The financial market began to unravel 40 years of a credit bubble combined with trillions of dollars of derivative investments. As a result, the future of investing will be substantially different than it was in the past. Investment expectations—particularly the 10% equity return assumption—have permanently changed for two generations of investors. We have turned 180 degrees and have transformed from a society of investors to a society of savers. People will, as a whole, work longer to receive the retirement they expected or will reduce their post-work expectations.

You must accept that you and most other investors lost a significant amount of money using asset allocation, the preferred investment and diversification solution of the financial services industry. Now, you must consider other investment strategies. Next, you must realize that financial planning and investment planning are actually two different things, and require different skill sets from practitioners. Therefore, it is mandatory to find an advisor who is competent in both categories, or else use two or more advisors. Also, you must note how much money you are paying to have your money managed, and determine whether the advice you receive is commensurate with the amount you spend.

You should certainly keep your current advisor if you are happy! But if you are not completely satisfied, determine why. Simply having a down year is no reason to fire an advisor—almost everyone lost money in 2008. However, good advisors should at least review your strategy to see if it is optimal in this new economic era. They should suggest tax loss harvesting strategies and continue to give advice. If your advisor has not done these things, consider finding a new one who understands different solutions for generating reasonable returns for your "Basic Needs" layer of investments, and knows how to invest properly for your other two (or more) layers. If your current advisor is unable to provide you with a customized, multi-tiered investment strategy, then start interviewing new ones as soon as possible.

How do you find advisors to interview? Getting referrals from trusted friends is always a good way to find advisors. Credentials also help, but you must be very careful about what they mean. A Chartered Life Underwriter (CLU) is an insurance industry designation. The CERTIFIED FINANCIAL PLANNER™ certification is the most recognized financial planning certification, but the investment advice taught in the course centers around "asset allocation" and not individual investment analysis. A Certified Investment Management Consultant (CIMC®) is knowledgeable about asset allocation and performance analysis and is useful for finding investments relative to others in various asset classes. Someone who has earned the Chartered Financial Analyst® designation (CFA®) is knowledgeable about both performance analysis and investment analysis. A CFA® charterholder must pass three rigorous all-day exams, given yearly. Many portfolio managers and analysts are CFA® charterholders. It is certainly the most difficult of the industry designations, but focuses little on financial planning. Note that it is now more common to find advisors with more than one industry designation, implying expertise in more than one area.

Advisors work on a commission, fee, or combination basis. If you are looking for comprehensive advice, avoid commission-based advisors, because their income is derived from selling products. Most insurance products sold today, including life insurance and annuities, are still commission-based even though the commission is often hidden and embedded within the return. Fee-based advisors charge hourly or flat fees for financial planning advice, or they charge fees for assets under management.

How much in fees should you pay an advisor? That depends upon what advice you receive, the returns you are seeking, and the quality of the advice. The industry norm of 1% per year for "asset allocation" on top of mutual fund and separate account management fees of 0.25% to 2.00% seems much too high to me. After all, we are in an environment (as of the writing of this book) where many asset classes are likely to return, on a best case scenario, 7% per year. You must, therefore, find a way to lower expenses to improve your returns.

There are several ways to lower your investment advisory fees and expenses. The first is to negotiate. I believe most advisors must lower their fees if their clients are to receive reasonable returns. Since they do not want to lose your business, negotiating with them may work. Note that this may be impossible for a "wirehouse" broker to do since fees are governed by the firm. The next way is to split the services provided by the advisor. Many advisors combine financial planning advice with their asset management. If you do not need financial planning advice, ask for that portion of their fee to be eliminated. Lastly, and most importantly, determine if you are receiving what you are paying for. Any "investment advisor" is a product salesperson and not an investment advisor if they are charging you 1% for keeping most of your investments inside a single fund family. If you do not need their financial planning advice, eliminate that fee by walking away and taking your investments with you.

Advisors charging 1% or more for a mass market "asset allocation" in a single fund family or asset allocation "product" should be avoided since that is something you can do yourself! Many of these advisors justify their fees by suggesting they are experts at choosing investment managers. As you already are painfully aware, most of these wealth managers did poorly during the market meltdown of 2008, the very time they were needed the most.

Please remember that trusted advisors offering customized advice should indeed be paid for their advice. A 1% fee can sometimes be justified, providing other services are provided. For example, if complicated financial or estate planning advice is not billed separately, a 1% fee may indeed be extremely fair and reasonable. Regardless, I believe most future asset management fees will drop well below 1%.

CHAPTER 18

CONCLUSION

Most financial advisors believe (or believed, as the case may now be) in "buy and hold" investing using a strategy called "asset allocation." This strategy was universally used by most financial advisors for nearly two decades during a time when the financial world was characterized by increasing financial leverage, increasing counterparty risk emanating from an out of control derivative market, rising stock prices, low volatility, the general acceptance of greedy Wall Street values, the tolerance of expensive investment products, an expectation of financially sound world governments, an expectation of future job security, and the expectation of 10% or better equity returns.

Asset allocation was a reasonable buy and hold strategy for managing money so long as history kept repeating itself. Only history did not repeat itself. When the balloon of financial leverage burst in 2008, asset prices quickly declined by historic amounts. This decline was the mother of all inflection points, permanently changing the way the world views financial leverage, financial derivatives, financial products, and asset valuation in a non-leveraged environment. It also altered how the world views job security, the definition of "full employment," the credit worthiness of financial governments, the propensity of the public to save, and the future returns we can expect from various asset classes.

As we are now painfully aware, buy and hold investing did not work very well over the past decade, and the assumptions behind the theory of traditional asset allocation failed. The "conventional wisdom" of the financial industry—asset allocation—did not adequately protect portfolios from dropping in value. These economic times are different from the past and require different strategies. This financial environment presents challenges to even the most seasoned investment professionals. Individual investors need a better method for managing money that is very different from what most advisors currently offer.

Individual clients in the post-2008 financial world need customized investment strategies that provide optimal solutions for their current and future needs. The rigid "asset allocation for every client" assumption used by most financial advisors should be abandoned for the multi-layered approach described in this book. Customization means having the flexibility to use various strategies, not just asset allocation, to meet objectives. Customization allows investors to take advantage of the investment vehicles that make the most sense at any given point in time. Customization allows investors to look anywhere for great investment opportunities.

Most advisors are not capable of managing money in a customized fashion. Many advisors do not have the experience and knowledge to do so. Other advisors cannot fit customized methods of asset management into their business model. Still others have broker/dealers who, for legal and compliance reasons, strongly prefer advisors to "asset allocate" all client accounts at the expense of customized advice.

There are many factors to be aware of and consider when investing in this lower return economic environment, including fraud, expectations for returns, asset valuations, financial products and fees.

This economy is fertile ground for dubious investment schemes, illegal scams, and fraud. Clearly, these must be avoided. Investors and their advisors must be diligent in thoroughly analyzing anything that sounds too good to be true.

The returns most investors can expect from real estate and equities will be lower than in the past. Valuations of financial assets will find new equilibriums, but it will be impossible to determine the normalized values for some time. Therefore, investor expectations should be lowered to reflect the "new normal."

Lowering the management costs of all portfolios is paramount in a lower return environment where equity returns may be one-third to one-half of what the conventional wisdom assumed in the last decade. Exchange traded funds will grow in popularity because of their liquidity and lower cost to buy and sell compared to many open-end mutual funds. Closed-end funds selling at discounts to their net asset value will replace many open-end funds in flexible portfolios because, all things being equal, they offer higher dividends than open-end funds selling at net asset value.

Managed accounts will still be popular, but the fees advisors charge for overseeing them will have to drop in view of lower expected returns. Hedge funds that actually hedge and fund of funds constructed properly will continue to attract investors. High net worth investors will demand concentrated portfolios of individual securities, and they will seek advisors who can provide this to them.

Over the next few years, there will be new financial products that should be considered for inclusion in flexible portfolios. Some of these products will specifically address the "Basic Needs" category of investing, carrying guarantees that allow investors to "sleep at night."

Investors will look at life insurance as protection and as a capital asset that should be reviewed on a regular basis. The lower return environment that I envision will make the guarantees of cash value life insurance currently available more valuable to the high net worth investor.

I believe the financial world will not come to an end as a result of the Great Recession that began in 2008. The chairman of the Federal Reserve and the world's finance ministers seem to understand the depth of the current crisis and are committed to finding practical solutions. One solution—printing money—will eventually be inflationary and/or result in higher taxes. At some point this will force investors to find different investment strategies to take these changes into account.

The good news for most high net worth investors is they already have the assets necessary to diversify and segregate their portfolios in the way I recommend in this book. In addition to providing reasonable expected returns, a customized and flexible portfolio allows you to take advantage of changing social, political and economic conditions in a way that asset allocation never could.

In the past, most advisors used a single strategy—asset allocation—for building portfolios for their high net worth clients. Building new portfolios that actually accomplish investor expectations will take more thought and competence than what was needed in the past. Some investors reading this book will be able to make strategic and tactical investment decisions by themselves. Bravo! Other investors should readily seek the help of competent financial professionals and investment advisors if they are unable or unwilling to tread the financial waters alone.

Most investors work hard to accumulate their money, and they expect their money to work hard for them. If you are like most investors, who experienced the markets of 2002, 2008 and 2011 when asset allocation was proven not to work, then you want something better. You now know that following the conventional wisdom or traditional asset allocation approach to investing worked better for the financial advisors, who sold the idea and received billions of dollars in fee income, than for the investors. Now there is a better solution that will work for you and help you prudently manage your assets regardless of the economic environment. By using the recommendations found in this book, you can construct portfolios that allow you to sleep at night and prosper over the days, months and years to come.

WORKS CITED

Ambachtsheer, Keith. "Beyond Portfolio Theory: The Next Frontier." *Financial Analysts Journal* 61.1 (2005): 29-33. Print.

Arnott, Robert D., and Frank J. Fabozzi. *Asset Allocation: a Handbook of Portfolio Policies, Strategies & Tactics.* Chicago, IL: Probus Pub., 1988. Print.

Arnott, Robert D., and Peter L. Bernstein. "What Risk Premium Is Normal?" *Financial Analysts Journal* 58.2 (2002): 64-85. Print.

Bernstein, Peter L. "Capital Ideas: From the Past to the Future." *Financial Analysts Journal* 61.6 (2005): 55-59. Print.

Bernstein, Peter L. "Overview: A Fifth Point of Inflection." *CFA Institute Conference Proceedings* 2004.1 (2004): 1-5. Print.

Bernstein, Peter L. "Points of Inflection: Investment Management Tomorrow." *Financial Analysts Journal* 59.4 (2003): 18-23. Print.

Birmingham, Stephen. *"Our Crowd": the Great Jewish Families of New York.* New York: Harper & Row, 1967. Print.

Bogle, John C. *Bogle on Mutual Funds: New Perspectives for the Intelligent Investor.* Burr Ridge, IL: Irwin, 1994. Print.

Brandes, Charles H. *Value Investing Today.* Homewood, IL: Dow Jones-Irwin, 1989. Print.

Ellis, Charles D. *Investment Policy: How to Win the Loser's Game.* Homewood, IL: Dow Jones-Irwin, 1985. Print.

Fabozzi, Frank J., Francis Gupta, and Harry M. Markowitz. "The Legacy of Modern Portfolio Theory." *The Journal of Investing* 11.3 (2002): 7-22. Print.

Fama, Eugene F., and Kenneth R. French. *Capital Asset Pricing Model: Theory and Evidence.* Chicago: Center for Research in Security Prices, Graduate School of Business, University of Chicago, 2004. Print.

Fama, Eugene F., and Merton H. Miller. *The Theory of Finance.* Montreal: Holt Rinehart et Winston, 1972. Print.

Geisst, Charles R. *Wall Street: a History: from Its Beginnings to the Fall of Enron.* Oxford: Oxford UP, 2004. Print.

Gibson, Roger C. *Asset Allocation: Balancing Financial Risk.* Chicago: Irwin Professional Pub., 1996. Print.

Harrington, Diana R. *Modern Portfolio Theory: the Capital Asset Pricing Model, and Arbitrage Pricing Theory: a User's Guide.* Englewood Cliffs: Prentice-Hall, 1987. Print.

Haugen, Robert A. *The New Finance: the Case against Efficient Markets.* Upper Saddle River, NJ: Prentice Hall, 1999. Print.

Hubbard, Jonathan. "The Legacy of Modern Portfolio Theory." *CFA Digest* 33.2 (2003): 50-52. Print.

Keel, Simon Theodor. *Optimal Portfolio Construction and Active Portfolio Management including Alternative Investments.* 2006. Print.

"Kenneth R. French - Data Library." *Tuck - MBA Program Web Server.* Web. 04 Feb. 2010. <http://mba.tuck.dartmouth.edu/pages/faculty/ken.french/data_library.html>.

Levy, Leon, and Eugene Linden. *The Mind of Wall Street.* New York: Public Affairs, 2002. Print.

Markowitz, Harry M. "Harry M. Markowitz - Prize Lecture." *Nobelprize.org.* The Nobel Foundation. Web. 28 Nov. 2010. <http://nobelprize.org/nobel_prizes/economics/laureates/1990/markowitz-lecture.html>.

Markowitz, Harry. *Portfolio Selection; Efficient Diversification of Investments.* New York: Wiley, 1959. Print.

Markowitz, Harry. "Portfolio Selection." *The Journal of Finance* 7.01 (1952): 77-91. Print.

Markowitz, Harry. "The Utility of Wealth." *The Journal of Political Economy* LX.2: 151-58. Print.

Modigliani, Franco, and Merton H. Miller. "The Cost of Capital, Corporation Finance and the Theory of Investment." *The American Economic Review* 48.3 (June, 1958): 261-97. Print.

Modigliani, Franco, and Merton Miller. "Corporate Income Taxes and the Cost of Capital: A Correction." *The American Economic Review* 53.3 (June, 1963): 433-43. Print.

Modigliani, Franco, Andrew B. Abel, and Simon Johnson. *The Collected Papers of Franco Modigliani.* Cambridge, MA: MIT, 1980. Print.

Perkins, Edwin J. *Wall Street to Main Street: Charles Merrill and Middle-class Investors.* Cambridge, Eng.: Cambridge UP, 1999. Print.

Prince, Russ Alan, and Karen File. *High-net-worth Psychology: Finding, Winning and Keeping Affluent Investors.* Fairfield, CT: HNW, 1999. Print.

Rudd, Andrew, and Henry K. Clasing. *Modern Portfolio Theory: the Principles of Investment Management.* Homewood, IL: Dow Jones-Irwin, 1982. Print.

Sander, Peter J. *Madoff: Corruption, Deceit, and the Making of the World's Most Notorious Ponzi Scheme.* Guilford, CT: Lyons, 2009. Print.

Sears, Steven M. "Seeking Safe Returns in a Perilous World." *BARRON'S* 3 Oct. 2009. Print.

Sharpe, William F. *AAT: Asset Allocation Tools.* Palo Alto, CA: Scientific, 1985. Print.

Sharpe, William F. *Portfolio Theory and Capital Markets.* New York: McGraw-Hill, 1970. Print.

Smithers, Andrew, and Stephen Wright. *Valuing Wall Street: Protecting Wealth in Turbulent Markets.* New York: McGraw-Hill, 2000. Print.

Soros, George. *The New Paradigm for Financial Markets: the Credit Crisis of 2008 and What It Means.* New York: PublicAffairs, 2008. Print.

Stewart, Scott D., John J. Neumann, Christopher R. Knittel, and Jeffrey Heisler. "Absence of Value: An Analysis of Investment Allocation Decisions by Institutional Plan Sponsors." *Financial Analysts Journal* 65.6 (2009): 34-51. Print.

Strauss, Lawrence C. "Krawcheck Stakes Her New Claim." *BARRON'S* 3 Oct. 2009, Feature sec. Print.

Tobin, James. "Money, Capital and Other Stores of Value." *The American Economic Review* 51.2 (May, 1961): 26-37. Print.

Train, John, and Thomas A. Melfe. *Investing and Managing Trusts under the New Prudent Investor Rule: a Guide for Trustees, Investment Advisors, and Lawyers.* Boston, MA: Harvard Business School, 1999. Print.

Vu, Joseph D.V. "Monetary Policy and the Cross-Section of Expected Stock Returns." *CFA Digest* 32.4 (2002): 27-28. Print.

Walker, Richard W. *The Development of Economic Thought on the Modigliani-Miller Theory of the Cost of Capital, Corporation Finance and the Theory of Investment.* 1982. Print.

Wilson, J. S. G. Money *Markets: the International Perspective.* London: Routledge, 1993. Print.

Zuckerman, By Gregory. "Fees, Even Returns and Auditor All Raised Flags - WSJ.com." *Business News & Financial News - The Wall Street Journal - WSJ.com.* Web. 28 Nov. 2010. <http://online.wsj.com/article/SB122910977401502369.html>.